The Spirit of the Common Law

Transaction Books by Roscoe Pound

Criminal Justice in America

An Introduction to the Philosophy of Law

Social Control Through Law

The Spirit of the Common Law

The Spirit of the Common Law

Roscoe Pound

with a new introduction by
Neil Hamilton &
Mathias Alfred Jaren

Transaction Publishers
New Brunswick (U.S.A.) and London (U.K.)

This book is printed on acid-free paper that meets the American National Standard for Permanence of Paper for Printed Library Materials.

Library of Congress Catalog Number: 98-24171
ISBN: 1-56000-942-X
Printed in the United States of America

Library of Congress Cataloging-in-Publication Data

Pound, Roscoe, 1870–1964.
The spirit of the common law / Roscoe Pound ; with a new introduction by Neil Hamilton and Mathias Alfred Jaren.
p. cm.
Originally published: Boston : Beacon Press, 1963.
Includes bibliographical references and index.
ISBN 1-56000-942-X (pbk. : alk. paper)
1. Common law—United States. 2. Common law—Philosophy. 3. Common law—History. I. Title.
KF394.P613 1998
340.5'7—dc21 98-24171
CIP

CONTENTS

INTRODUCTION TO THE TRANSACTION EDITION

NATHAN ROSCOE POUND was born in Nebraska on October 27, 1870. The Pound family was deeply rooted in American history, even by the 1870s. John Pound had arrived from England two centuries before to settle in the Delaware valley of Pennsylvania-New Jersey in 1648. Receiving a grant under William Penn's colonial charter, John Pound became a successful farmer, working a portion of land lying in what was then "West Jersey." Roscoe Pound referred to his ancestor as "a devoted man of conscience. . . . [I]n the violent conflicts of his day, the teachings of plain speaking and truth telling and worthy living with the avoidance of the vanities of heraldry and of war spoke to him imperatively."[1] Roscoe's Father, Stephen Bosworth Pound, began practicing law in New York in 1863. Along with his new wife, Laura Biddlecombe, he emigrated to the Nebraska prairie in 1866, thus joining in the formation of the State of Nebraska in 1867, and witnessing the beginnings of the University of Nebraska a year before Roscoe's birth, in 1869.

The Pound family's Quaker roots appeared in subtle themes throughout Roscoe Pound's life. In commenting to his first biographer, Paul Sayre,

Pound disclaimed a few sentences Sayre had written, with a ringing assertion: "Why pay any attention to what 'captios and petty persons' say? It has been my invariable rule to ignore personal attacks, to try to understand rather than criticize, and to respond to critics by discussion of the subject rather than by polemics as to their views."[2] Pound has no recorded collection of great detractors, yet to one uncovered by Sayre, Pound again emphasized: "I had anticipated worse from the *Harvard Law Review* which has usually sent my books to what I would call unfriends. But it has been my inflexible rule never to answer attacks. Since in time the attacks are forgotten."

During Sayre's work on Roscoe's biography published in 1948, Olivia Pound, a sister, was to tell Sayre, "[W]e are never in our family disturbed by criticism. When Louise's first book, an epoch making one it proved to be, came out, some Harvard reviewer said it was the maunderings of a disordered mind."[3] Louise Pound, a second sister, taught for years at Swarthmore College in Pennsylvania. Roscoe joined the Hicksite Quaker Meeting at Swarthmore, and according to Sayre, "he did quite definitely take the view that perhaps the heart of the Society of Friends was in their emphasis on conduct and 'spirit' or 'inner light,' not upon theological or superhuman dogmas."[4] Reading *The Spirit of the Common Law*, one will see, albeit at all times quite subtle, Pound's search for the spirit of humankind in legal reasoning. Pound sought a paradigm through which individuals could reach their most enlightened terms of human existence.

Pound explored the development of the law, particularly themes of individual rights, in various literatures, starting with law's western origins in Roman discourse, through the evolution of English common law, the development of the French codes, and the early law of the colonies, built by people who borrowed from earlier legacies. He brought to bear a unique and enormous range of inquiry and knowledge in the sciences, the humanities and the social sciences. New York University Dean Arthur Vanderbilt observed that:

> Mr. Justice Holmes, with his customary felicity of phrasing, was driven to coin a word to describe Roscoe Pound, whom he most appropriately characterized as "uniquity." Roscoe Pound is not only one of the rare encyclopedic minds of the law and the surrounding social sciences, but by common consent our most widely known American Jurist, past or present; he has always made his unique catholicity of interests and his astounding depth of erudition serve the common cause. A pioneer in American procedural reform, the guiding genius of the Cleveland Crime Survey, vigorous opponent of administrative absolutism and Founder of the School of Sociological Jurisprudence, he has brought to each successive task of law reform the resources of both the common law

> and the civil law and the disciplines of the several social sciences.[5]

The "catholicity" Dean Vanderbilt attributed to Pound was not something Pound would say about Mr. Justice Holmes. Writing to Paul Sayre, Pound commented:

> I quite agree with you that there has been a deal of nonsense written of late about Mr. Justice Holmes. It is the fashion for everybody with any sort of wild idea to try to attach it to Holmes' memory. He certainly was an outstanding figure among American judges and American legal scholars. At the same time, it must be confessed that his work was somewhat unequal. He was by no means good on questions of criminal law, for a long time he had notions about equity derived from Massachusetts where equity was very behind hand in its development, and for a long time he somewhat obstinately held to the notion that negligence could be reduced to a body of detailed rules. In other words, even Homer sometimes nodded. I am afraid that by way of reaction from the extravagant stuff that has been written about him of late he may come to be unappreciated in the next generation.[6]

Roscoe Pound was no less critical about himself. Reflecting one evening while penning a letter to a dear friend after an arduous day of practicing law, Pound asked, "Why am I in the law? Why because my father wished it. Why do I make a pretense of being civilized when I am at heart one of the most uncivilized creatures at large?"[7] Study of the law was actually Pound's second choice. Pound started his academic career seriously engaged in the study of botany at the University of Nebraska, receiving his B.A. in 1888.

Pound became a student at Harvard Law School in 1889. Harvard Law School is aptly characterized in this period from letters between law school professor John Chipman Gray[8] and Harvard's president, Charles Eliot: "The idols of the cave which a school bred lawyer is sure to substitute for the facts, may be much better material for intellectual gymnastics than the facts themselves and may call forth more enthusiasm in the pupils, but a school where the majority of the professors shuns and despises the contact with actual facts has got the seeds of ruin in it and will and ought to go to the devil."[9] Christopher Columbus Langdell was then dean of Harvard Law School. David Wigdor, writing a 1974 biography on Roscoe Pound, refers to Langdell's educative system as a "catholicity of science: in drawing upon English as well as American reports for the development of legal principles."[10] The case method introduced by Langdell required students to read and discuss cases, using inductive reasoning to derive for themselves the principles of the law.

Langdell was not to have enraptured all of his fellow scholars. Oliver Wendell Holmes, Jr., believed that Langdell's *Elements of Contract* was "a misspent piece of marvelous ingenuity," and that Langdell himself represented "the powers of darkness."[11] Holmes goes on in a 1908 letter to Sir Frederick Pollack writing that Langdell's *Equity Jurisdiction* displays "the narrow side of his mind, his feebleness in philosophising, and hints at his rudimentary historical knowledge. I think he (Langdell) is somewhat wanting in horsesense."[12]

The year 1889 was an exciting year for Pound, but Harvard and Boston were not yet to become a central source of gratification to him. He left law study after one year at Harvard, returning to Nebraska to practice law and to go back to his botanical inquiries.

These years from 1890 to 1900 were a mixture of botanical study and law practice with his father. Pound pleaded his first Nebraska jury case in 1893 against another rising star in American justice, William Jennings Bryan.[13] By 1896 he entered the world of contributing authors to legal periodicals by publishing "Dogs and the Law." In a humorous comment on the common law and treatises, Pound observed, "The barbarous doctrines of the common law which did not make dog-stealing larceny will come in for vigorous invective."[14] Pound rages on, "I trust enough has been said to indicate the field which lies open for some industrious author and enterprising publisher. The profession will wait impatiently for a Treatise on Canine Jurisprudence. . . . May I hope that these suggestions will be rewarded by a presentation copy of the two volumes when issued? I fear not, such is human ingratitude, unless I can outdo the regular writers of testimonials and reviews for circular publication, and furnish the enterprising publisher aforesaid *quid pro quo*."[15]

Pound continued to study botany and earned his Ph.D. in 1897 while serving as the director of the Nebraska Botanical Survey. He also practiced during the decade, taught "adjunct" in the new state law school at Lincoln, and in 1901 was appointed judge to the Nebraska Supreme Court.

In an early opinion, Pound wrote: "The theory of our system is that the law consists not in the actual rules enforced by decisions of the courts at any one time, but the principles from which these rules flow; that old principles are applied to new cases, and the rules resulting from such application are modified from time to time as changed conditions and new states of fact require."[16] This judicial opinion of the law as stated in 1903 was a central theme which Pound would explore often. He became the dean of the University of Nebraska Law School the same year, a position in which Pound would continue to develop his own ideas and philosophies of law.

Writing in 1905,[17] Pound set forth the first thesis of his view of "mechanical jurisprudence," using the law of equity as a backdrop. Pound brought a personal pragmatism to bear in analyzing the decadence he discovered in the law of equity. Reflecting on his former colleague, Albert Kocourk described Pound: "Somewhat like Holmes, Pound's plan of life was simple—tackle the thing before you and get what you can out of it. A metaphysician might object that this represents no genuine philosophy, and that it is not a demonstrable counsel of perfection. However that may be, the formula is one that works, and that is all that pragmatism requires.[18]

Understanding Pound's pragmatism is a significant task, but Sayre provided a useful summary in his 1947 collection of essays on Pound.[19] A cogent and brief characterization is offered by Thomas Cowan, a former colleague of Pound's:

> The burden of all pragmatic philosophy is that to arrive at final truth is fatal. But equally fatal is failure to know whether our striving brings us nearer or farther from the truth. In a word, our task is to define truth in such a way that, although we must never arrive at it, yet we must be able to approach it indefinitely. Truth becomes an unattainable, indefinitely approachable ideal. And the philosophy of science is the working out of the conditions of this ideal in the form of a fruitful methodology for science. We accept then the fundamental tenet of pragmatism. No generalization or law remains final. It becomes fact or datum in the further pursuit of truth. No fact is final. Its meaning becomes absorbed in law or generalization. There is no fixed starting point for science. Neither rational intuitions nor the data of experience are the unalterable first beginnings of knowl-

> edge. Any intuition, whether rational or sensuous, may serve as a starting point. So much for the expansive power of the pragmatic insight.[20]

David Wigdor, Pound's second biographer, writing in 1974, a decade after Pound's death, takes a more critical view regarding Pound's jurisprudence:

> Pound earned a reputation during the Progressive era as one of the most innovative American legal theorists, but his commitment to the common law fostered a fascination with organicism, traditionalism, and professionalism that restricted his intellectual range. His creativity, checked by internal contradictions, was spent upon peculiarities. The separate instrumental and organic elements of his thought, developed in isolation, created an unresolved dualism within his jurisprudence and made it impossible for him to develop the grand system that he pursued so assiduously.[21]

Wigdor's picture of Pound gives insufficient weight to the merger of pragmatism and Pound's own intellectual power and range that makes Pound's scholarship on the common law so interesting.[22] Pound's contemporaries credit him with exceptional intellectual range. "Holmes said of Pound, 'The number of things that chap knows drives me silly.' Pollock says, 'He seems to have read every mortal thing published in English, French, and German about the philosophy of law, besides a vast mass of reported cases.'" Pollock, to whom Holmes had given a letter of introduction, spoke of him (Pound) as "monstrously learned" and as "the learned and ingenious Pound."[23]

The "ingenious" Pound to which Pollock refers can be explored in reflections and comments among Pound's early writings. Reading Pound's early major works reveals several analytical contexts. The analysis of cases was antecedent to the comparative exploration of doctrinal materials in the treatises. In his 1905 article titled "The Decadence of Equity," Pound tested the generalizations of the treatises by careful analysis of the case law, looking at doctrinal shifts in equity and procedure. This technique rendered meaningless the generalizations made by the text writers, and Pound concluded that the text writers state the exception far too broadly, and ignore the general rule.[24]

In the 1905 article, Pound, experienced as a practicing lawyer, judge, and law school dean, formed strong opinions. "[L]aws are general rules recognized or enforced in the administration of justice. But the very fact that laws are general rules, based on abstraction and the disregard of the variable and less material elements in affairs, makes them mechanical in their operation. A mechanism is bound in nature to act mechanically, and not according to the requirements of a particular case."[25] Here Pound introduced a major analytical paradigm he would often revisit. Pound's scientific thinking as a botanist led him to see plant organisms in their various forms as having both specific mechanistic functions, yet also limitations. By analogy, Pound observed a paradigm of mechanistic rules of law, subject to boundaries or limitations.

"Abstract general rules" became "bound in nature," existing at fixed points, having finite applications and limitations. The concept led one effectively into the second dimension in the argument, where Pound addressed the "requirements of a particular case." Individuals as adversaries have unique problems that cannot be reconciled using legal prescriptions, which over decades have assimilated into doctrinal views. The "Decadence" to which Pound referred was the use by legal professionals of classical maxims in equity in place of rigorous thinking to solve individual legal conflicts. Certainly Pound would be pleased to conclude this idea with his own statement: "So soon as a system of law becomes reduced to completeness of outward form, it has a natural tendency to crystallize into a rigidity unsuited to the free applications which the actual circumstances of human life demand. . . . We are dealing, however, with the present and immediate future. . . . Commercial and industrial development, as Montesquieu saw in his day, make for certainty. The commercial world demands rules. No man makes large investments trusting to uniform exercise of discretion."[26]

The year 1905 was a banner year for Pound; *Co-*

lumbia Law Review took two of his articles. The second was an article in which Pound asked the legal community, "Do We Need a Philosophy of Law?"[27] This article presented the second major construct in Pound's thinking, one that predates the 1921 *Spirit of the Common Law* by sixteen years. Pound's work over these decades is testimony to the time it takes for the germination and development of ideas. In 1905 Pound declared:

> To-day, for the first time, the common law finds itself arrayed against the people; for the first time, instead of securing for them what they most prize, they know it chiefly as something that continually stands between them and what they desire. It cannot be denied that there is a growing popular dissatisfaction with our legal system. . . . No amount of admiration for our traditional system should blind us to the obvious fact that the law exhibits too great a respect for the individual, and for the intrenched position in which our legal and political history has put him, and too little respect for the needs of society, when they come in conflict with the individual, to be in touch with the present age.[28]

Pound's analysis and argument examined the wage and hour laws, citing nine cases which culminated in the judicial holding that labor rights in the context of eight-hour laws were unconstitutional.[29] Pound's analysis predated by three years the famous "Brandeis Brief" used in the arguments before the U.S. Supreme Court in *Muller v. State of Oregon*.[30]

Pound opposed the constitutional use of individual rights to obstruct stabilization of labor interests in America's growing industrial society. At the beginning of the twentieth century, the notion of individual rights took on a very different form than readers entering the twenty-first century might conclude. After reviewing nine labor-related court decisions, Pound explained: "I do not criticize these decisions. As the law stands, I do not doubt they were rightly determined. But they serve to show that the right of the individual to contract as he pleases is upheld by our legal system at the expense of the right of society to stand between our laboring population and oppression." Constitutional limitations on government supervision over contracts did not sit well with Pound: "This right of the individual and this exaggerated respect for his right are common-law doctrines. And this means that a struggle is in progress between society and the common law; for the judicial power over unconstitutional legislation is on the right line of common law ideas."[31] To reinforce this view, Pound emphasized several dramatic arguments:

1. "Today the isolated individual is no longer taken for the center of the universe."
2. "We see now that he is an abstraction, and has never had a concrete existence."
3. "Today, we look instead for liberty through society. We no longer hold that society exists entirely for the sake of the individual."

4. "The common law, however, is concerned, not with social righteousness, but with individual rights."[32]

Pound concluded: "The common law, in the interest of the individual, is struggling with the prerogatives of the people, represented by the police power, as it struggled with a like prerogative of the crown from Henry VII to James II."[33]

In this second article Pound traced English law, and by historical argument illustrated the tenacity of the common law. He then drew the conclusion that the tension over economic rights of individuals who occupy vastly different positions in the financial strata can be reconciled within common law judicial reasoning and constitutional police powers. This tension according to Pound "is furnishing the antidote for the intense regard for the individual which our legal system exhibits. . . .[In] fact a progressive liberalizing of our constitutional law is noticeable already, and to all appearance, a slow but sure change of front is in progress."[34] The "progressive liberalizing" Pound observed in his world at the beginning of the twentieth century must be tempered: for "the residuary power is ill defined, and the common law is jealous of all indefinite power."[35] Interpolating from these developments in constitutional and common law, Pound in 1905 asked the crucial question of the twentieth century: "How shall we lead our law to hold a more even balance between individualism and socialism?" This is another question he will often visit in his writings. In this article, his first answer: "To my mind, the remedy is in our law schools. It is in training the rising generation of lawyers in a social, political and legal philosophy abreast of our time."[36]

Pound published a short article in 1906 bearing the same name as the collection of essays you are about to read, "The Spirit of the Common Law."[37] This is an extremely important article, one which should be read in its entirety along with the set of lectures from 1921. In 1906, Pound concluded: "Nothing in the history of our common law is more striking than its tenacity in holding ground." "Not only has the common law as a system successfully resisted all attempts to bring in some other law in its place, but in those parts of our system where alien and more flexible methods have existed or have arisen, in contravention of the fundamental theory of the common law that litigation is contentious, and wherever arbitrary discretion has obtained a serious foothold, the common law has ultimately prevailed."[38] Pound added, "An achievement strictly in line with the history of the common law is the intrenchment of its doctrines [particularly regarding individual rights] in our constitutions, state and federal, culminating in the Fourteenth Amendment, so that its fundamental and distinctive dogmas are beyond the reach of ordinary state action, and are to be dislodged in many cases only by amendment of the Federal Constitution itself."[39] Pound sought to capture the critical characteristics of the common law.

Three characteristics set off the common law system from all others:

1. the supremacy of law;
2. case law and precedent; and
3. contentious procedure.

These are defined and grounded in their historical origins:

> The supremacy of the law—the doctrine that all questions may be tried in the course of orderly litigation between individuals, and that no person and no act is beyond law—is the Germanic principle that the state is bound to act by law.
>
> Our doctrine of precedents is almost as old. The first precedents were writs, and Glanvill's book is a collection of them. Bracton relied on the judgment rolls, and his Note Book is something like a report. . . . Contentious procedure is Germanic, and characterizes English law from before the Conquest.
>
> [T]hese three doctrines resolve themselves to a fundamental proposition that law exists for individuals, and hence is to deal with every question as a contest between individuals, is to decide it on its individual facts, not arbitrarily, but as like cases have been adjudged for

others, and is to allow the parties to fight out the contest for themselves, and as much as possible in their own way.[40]

The problem, therefore, of the present is to lead our law to hold a more even balance between individualism and collectivism. Its present extreme individualism must be tempered to meet the ideas of a modern world. . . .We must revert for a season to the residuary power of the *parens patriae* to do justice. The power of rejuvenescence, inherent in our legal system, must be invoked. We must cease to mistake seventeenth century dogmas, in which temporary phases of its individualist bent were formulated, for fundamental tenets of the common law.[41]

As dean of Nebraska's fledgling law school, Pound expanded his forum. A speech given to the Nebraska Bar Association gave rise to an invitation to Pound to present before the American Bar Association Meeting in 1906 in St. Paul, Minnesota.[42] The speech was well described by John Wigmore,[43] present that summer evening:

Some 370 members (ABA total membership in 1905 was 5,400) were registered for the convention, and almost all of them (with many of their ladies) were present in the spacious auditorium of the Capitol.

The title of the address was "The Causes of Popular Dissatisfaction with the Administration of Justice." The speaker was a youngish lawyer in his early thirties, a local light in Nebraska—brought on this national stage simply because the Association's president had recently heard him speak at a meeting of the Nebraska Bar Association. The speaker opened with the concession that dissatisfaction with the administration of justice is as old as law, and quoted examples from past history. But he proceeded promptly to assert that there was today in our own country "more than the normal amount of dissatisfaction with the present day administration of justice in America." Then, limiting his inquiry to civil justice (which was a preliminary jolt to the conservatives—for of course that was their special field of practice), he proceeded to a diagnosis of those causes. And herein came the first recorded instance of the philosophic approach; for he classified the causes under four heads—from greater to less, from permanent to changeable:

(1) Causes for dissatisfaction with any legal system;
(2) Causes lying in the peculiarities of our Anglo-American legal system;
(3) Causes lying in our American judicial organization and procedure; and
(4) Causes lying in the environment of our judicial administration.

Here the speech came to its main thesis, a concrete bill of particular defects, then the conservative hearers sat in dumb dismay and hostile horror at the deliverances of the daring iconoclast (all phrased, nonetheless, in coldly calm description).

"Our system of courts is archaic." "Our procedure is behind the times." "Our judicial power is wasted." "The worst feature of procedure is the lavish granting of new

> trials." "The court's time is frittered away on mere points of legal etiquette." "Our legislation is crude." "Putting courts into politics had almost destroyed the traditional respect for the Bench!"[44]

The audience reactions ranged from the outraged to the highly interested; while there were many critics and detractors, Pound had correctly calculated the balance. The 1906 speech was for years considered a landmark, and turning point in how many of the members of the legal profession perceived themselves. Thirty years after the speech, Wigmore wrote:

> Whenever the question is mooted of the progress of reform in our administration of civil justice—whenever may be heard impatience at the profession's too-leisurely speed, let this be remembered, that it all started after the speech at St. Paul. That speech made history. At that period there was universal complacent torpidity in the profession; the thermometer of conscious progressive and collective effort was at freezing point. The rise of its temperature has all taken place in the last thirty years.[45]

Following the 1906 speech, Pound's academic career rapidly developed. Dean Wigmore of Northwestern, captivated by Pound's speech the previous year in St. Paul, recruited Pound to join the faculty at Northwestern. In 1909 Pound moved to the University of Chicago to teach law. During this period the articles continued. An article appeared in 1907 entitled "Executive Justice."[46] Pound built on a theme articulated in the 1906 speech that adverse public reaction to the common law's doctrine of supremacy of law, which tied down administration by common law liabilities and judicial review, had resulted in the creation of executive boards with summary and plenary powers, freed from judicial review. In the article Professor Pound identified a paralysis in the administration of justice: What is this paralysis of administration? Pound tells us that, "[T]he recrudescence of executive justice is gaining strength continually and is yet far from its end."[47] The disease to which Pound referred is what he observed in annual reports of the American Bar Association. "From fifteen to twenty statutes giving wide powers of dealing with the liberty or property of citizens to executive boards, to be exercised summarily, or upon such hearing as comports with lay notions of fair play, may be seen enumerated in the reviews of current legislation in each of the last ten reports of the American Bar Association."[48]

In his search for an explanation, Pound stated: "Perhaps the beginning of judicial acquiescence in a departure from the common-law jealousy of arbitrary executive action is coincident with the general introduction of an elective judiciary. Certainly the submissiveness of elected judges under legislative encroachments upon the judicial department has been well marked." To Pound the role of the judiciary had been substantially weakened, and he illustrated this, stating: "our appellate courts have acquiesced in legislation prescribing how and when they shall write opinions and give reasons for their decisions. Even more, the trial judges in a majority of our commonwealths have been shorn of their just powers of advising the jury and have been reduced to mere umpires, in the interest of unfettered forensic display: and no protest has been heard."[49] Pound did not see this shift from judicial control over to administrative boards to be caused by life's complexity or the division of labor. Rather "we see in this recrudescence of executive justice one of those reversions to justice without law which are perennial in legal history and serve, whenever a legal system fails for the time being to fulfil its purpose, to infuse into it enough of current morality to preserve its life."[50]

To Pound, "Executive justice is an evil. It has always been and it always will be crude and as variable as the personalities of officials." The origins of executive justice, in Pound's historical assessment, were the courts of equity in Rome and England. Equity courts "acted without rule in accordance with general notions of fair play and sympathy for the weaker party. The law was not fulfilling its end; it was not adjusting the relations of individuals with each other so as to accord with the moral sense of the community."[51] Pound collapsed the problem into a sense of the vogue. "Summary administrative action becomes the fashion. An elective judiciary, sensitive to the public will, blithely yields up its prerogatives, and the return to a government of men is achieved." Thus, Pound concluded: "[I]f we are to preserve the common law doctrine of supremacy of law, the profession and the courts must take up vigorously and fearlessly the problem of to-day—how to *administer* the law to meet the demands of the world that is" (original emphasis).[52]

Pound finished a second article in 1907, "Spurious Interpretations."[53] This article was Pound's view of legal analysis. It is as fitting for what we call statutory interpretation now as it was in 1907. The particular value this article retains is Pound's exposition of legal analysis in contexts of human moral reasoning. Pound, borrowing from Austin's essay on interpretation,[54] saw two dimensions to interpretation. "The former means of interpretation tries to find out directly what the law-maker meant by assuming his position, in the surroundings in which he acted, and endeavoring to gather from the mischiefs he had to meet and the remedy by which he sought to meet them, his intention with respect to the particular point in controversy." In the alternative, "[I]f the former fails to yield sufficient light, (one) seeks to reach the intent of the law-maker indirectly." Pound here alluded to the "*reason and spirit of the rule*, or to the intrinsic merit of the several possible interpretations" (emphasis added).[55] This type of "Spurious interpretation reintroduces the personal element into the administration of justice. The whole aim of law is to get rid of this element. And however popular arbitrary judicial action and raw equity may be for a time, nothing is more foreign to the public interest, and more certain in the end to engender disrespect if not hatred for the law."[56] Thus, Pound concluded, "Over-rigid constitutions, carelessly drawn statutes, and legislative indifference toward purely legal questions are not permanently remedied by wrenching the judicial system to obviate their mischievous effects. As the sins of the judicial department are compelling an era of executive justice, the sins of popular and legislative law-making are threatening to compel a return to an era of judicial law-making."[57]

It was also 1907 when Pound published an article entitled "The Need of a Sociological Jurisprudence."[58] The article illustrates Pound's search for a position from which he can infuse scholarship and clear thinking into lawmaking, which, in Pound's view, had become "mechanical." In the heyday of the Industrial Revolution, Pound suggested that men were thinking like machines. Enormous industrial collectives demanded and received legal and government protections, for example, making them into artificial individuals, and using that legal fiction spuriously for the alleged benefit of all citizens.[59] Pound sensed this acutely, "[I]t must be admitted that the law of the land has not the real hold upon the American people which law should have, and that there is a growing tendency to insist upon individual standards and to apply them in the teeth of the collective standard which is or ought to be expressed in the law." Pound argued that this is true based on a review of ninety cases from the National Reporter System. The cases involved actions against employers for personal injuries. Pound found: "[I]t is notorious that a crude and ill-defined sentiment that employers and great industrial enterprises should bear the cost of the human wear and tear incident to their operations, dictates more verdicts than the rules of law laid down in the charges of the courts."[60] Pound was sympathetic to a comment by labor leader Samuel Gompers that "he would obey no injunction that deprived him of his rights." Pound commented that "Much of this individual self-assertion against the law is due, no doubt, to the lack of a settled social standard of justice during a period of transition. But a large part must be attributed to a wide-spread disrespect for law, to a general sentiment that unless the individual does so assert himself, he or those in whom he feels an interest will not be dealt with as justice requires."[61]

Legal education in 1907 loomed as a core problem to Pound: "So long as the one object is to train practitioners who can make money at the Bar, and so long as schools are judged chiefly by their success in affording such training, we may expect nothing better . . . they are not bound to teach traditional legal pseudo-science."[62] Quite to the point, Pound was to become dean of Harvard Law School in 1916, and one wonders how many Harvard faculty saw this 1907 remark: "Legal monks who pass their lives in an atmosphere of pure law, from which every worldly and human element is excluded, cannot shape practical principles to be applied to a restless world of flesh and blood."[63] The call for action resounded in the article: "It is, therefore, the duty of American teachers of law to investigate the sociological foundations, not of law alone, but of the common law and of the special topics in which they give instruction, and, while teaching the actual law by which courts decide, to give to their teaching the color which will fit new generations of lawyers to lead the people as they should, instead of giving up their legitimate hegemony in legislation and politics to engineers and naturalists and economists."[64]

In 1910, Harvard Law School appointed Pound to the Story Professorship. In 1911, Pound published "The Scope and Purpose of Sociological Jurisprudence" in *Harvard Law Review*.[65] Pound again advocated analyzing law using political, economic, and other social sciences. New social science knowledge could assist courts in adjusting our common law tradition to contemporary social conditions. Pound's pragmatism led also to further emphasis on the balance necessary between legislative rules and the common law.

> Experience has shown abundantly that rule and order in the administration of justice are best attained by making it possible to measure relations and situations, as they become the subjects of controversy, by reason. To a certain extent, the will of society as to the relations of individuals with each other may be ascertained and declared in advance. . . . For the great mass of causes, the ideals of uniformity and certainty are to be reached by requiring and permitting the magistrate to bring to bear upon them a trained reason and an enlightened, disciplined sense of justice.[66]

In a 1912 article, "Theories of Law," published in *Yale Law Journal*, Pound returned again to the theme that the common law, which Pound referred to as the traditional element, and legislative rules, which Pound referred to as the enacted or imperative element, are closely interrelated. Over time, Pound explained, as judicial experience develops the common law into clear principles, these principles are incorporated into legislative rules, which in the process of time become absorbed into the legal system and are themselves interpreted and developed by the common law, which fills the gaps in legislation and further develops the principles of legislation.[67] In 1913, Pound observed in "The Administration of

Justice in the Modern City" that the common law or traditional element of the law was clearly undergoing change: "Gradually the traditional element of our law is absorbing and being made over by the economics and social science of to-day."[68]

Pound also revisited the "increasing apparatus of commissions, board and inspectors . . . to meet the needs of our great urban communities" in "The Administration of Justice in the Modern City." Pound recognized that the heterogeneous communities in modern cities posed difficulties for the common law. The common law polity presupposed "a homogeneous population, which is jealous of its rights, zealous to enforce law and order, and in sympathy with the law and with the institutions of government."[69] Because of the demands of the modern city, justice requires a "more thorough knowledge of the social conditions in our cities, for which law must be devised and to which it must be applied. We must have sociological teaching and study of the law and of the theories upon which law shall proceed."[70]

Pound became dean at Harvard Law School in 1916, a position in which he would remain for twenty years. He continued publishing and giving lectures, bringing together and developing the themes introduced in his earlier writing. He was fifty-one when the collection of lectures given at Dartmouth College, *The Spirit of the Common Law*, was first published in 1921.

The book is both a celebration of the common law and a warning for common law judges and lawyers to return to and embrace the pragmatism and judicial empiricism that define and energize the common law. The two fundamental doctrines of the common law, Pound wrote, were the doctrine of precedents and the doctrine of supremacy of law.

> The doctrine of precedents means that causes are to be judged by principles reached inductively from the judicial experience of the past, not by deduction from rules established arbitrarily by the sovereign will. In other words, reason, not arbitrary will, is to be the ultimate ground of decision. The doctrine of supremacy of law is reducible to the same idea. It is a doctrine that the sovereign (whether king, legislature or the electorate) and all its agencies are bound to act on principles, not according to arbitrary will: are obliged to follow reason instead of being free to follow caprice. . . .The common-law doctrine is one of reason applied to experience. It assumes that experience will afford the most satisfactory foundation for standards of action and principles of decision. It holds that law is not to be arbitrarily decided by a fiat of the sovereign will, but it is to be discovered by judicial and juristic experience of the rules and principles which in the past have accomplished or failed to accomplish justice. . . . [W]e must find in the criticism of the reported decision by bench and bar . . . our assurance that they will be governed by reason and that the personal equation of the individual judge will be suppressed.[71]

The doctrine of precedents, Pound concluded, combines certainty with the potential for growth in a way that no other approach to law has achieved. "Certainty is insured within reasonable limits in that the court proceeds by analogy of rules and doctrines . . . and develops a principle for the cause before it according to a known technique. Growth is insured in that the limits of the principle are not fixed authoritatively once and for all but are discovered gradually by a process of inclusion and exclusion as cases arise which bring out its practical workings and prove how far it may be made to do justice in its actual operation."[72]

The common law tradition, Pound argued, had two principal historical characteristics:

1. Common law courts established that there were fundamental common law rights of the English people which individuals might maintain in courts and which the courts would secure, even against the king. By natural transition, common law limitations on the king's authority become limitations on all authority.[73] Because the common law gave effect to individual natural rights against other individuals and particularly the state, it is characterized by an extreme individualism in terms of an unlimited valuation of individual liberty and respect for individual property. It is concerned not with general social welfare but with individual rights. It tries questions of the highest social impact as mere controversies

between two parties. Its respect for the individual makes procedure ultra contentious. It is so zealous to secure fair play for the individual that it secures little fair play for the public.

2. On the other hand, the common law is also characterized by an element going in the other direction. It deals with people in groups, classes or relations, like landlord/tenant, principal/agent, or mortgagor/mortgagee, in order to establish consistent principles.[74]

The common law came under public indictment in the United States at the turn of the century. Its doctrine of supremacy of law and consequent judicial power over unconstitutional legislation was too protective of individual rights of liberty and property in a society rapidly changing to become more heterogeneous, complex, urban, and industrial.[75] The urban public demanded greater recognition of the rights of the people, not just individual rights. The older generation of lawyers and judges believed the principles of the common law to be absolute and eternal, and forgot its roots in pragmatism and judicial empiricism.[76] This put the common law in tension with public desire.

The public's loss of confidence in overly strict decisions by common law courts, Pound feared, was driving the society quickly toward administrative justice through boards and commissions with loosely defined powers, unlimited discretion, and inadequate judicial restraints.[77] This, Pound believed, was a reversion to justice without supremacy of law in the form of "administrative tribunals in which the relations of individuals with each other and with the state were adjusted summarily according to the notions for the time being of an administrative officer as to what the general interest or good conscience demanded, unencumbered by many rules."[78]

Pound urged that a body of law that will satisfy the demands of society at the turn of the century could not be made out of the ultra-individualistic materials of nineteenth-century common law. He urged common law lawyers and courts to remember the common law's roots in pragmatism, judicial empiricism, and creative problem solving and to turn to new ideas from the social sciences for new premises and ideas in such form that the court may use them and develop them into a modern system by judicial experience of actual causes.[79] "It is agreed that the path of deliverance from the stagnation of nineteenth-century law is a judicial empiricism, working upon the materials supplied by jurist and legislator."[80]

The history of the twentieth century confirms Pound's prescience concerning the growth of the fourth branch of government, the administrative agencies, into the modern administrative state. At the end of this century, administrative agencies in rule making or adjudication are making the substantial majority of laws in the United States. A major task of twentieth-century jurisprudence has been how to hold unelected agency administrators accountable to the people when the Constitution, the fundamental document outlining the relationships both among the branches of government and of the government to the people, has almost nothing to say about agencies.

Pound's hope was that common law courts could use judicial empiricism to work upon the materials supplied by jurist and legislator to reestablish the supremacy of law over administrative agencies. Supremacy of law demands that the sovereign and all its agencies are bound to act on principles, not according to arbitrary will, and are obliged to follow reason instead of being free to follow caprice. In 1946, Congress enacted the Administrative Procedure Act (the APA), providing for judicial review of agency rule making and adjudication to determine if the agency action is both lawful and not arbitrary, capricious or an abuse of discretion. The federal courts, interpreting the broad terms of judicial review within the APA, have created a rich common law of judicial review, particularly the hard look doctrine requiring substantial agency findings and reasons for agency action. Supremacy of law was again victorious.

The history of the twentieth century also confirms both Pound's prediction that the common law would absorb and be made over by the social sciences and

Pound's hope that law professors would investigate and teach the social science foundations of law, especially the common law.

The Brandeis brief, which marshals social science data, expert opinion, and historical experience to support a legal opinion, is now commonplace. The law and economics school of legal analysis originating at the University of Chicago has had a major impact on judicial opinions, legislation, and agency decision making. Forms of cost benefit analysis are common. Many law professors now have advanced degrees in both law and other disciplines, and both law school curricula and legal scholarship are strongly interdisciplinary. Pound might have wondered whether the movement toward interdisciplinary study of law has gone too far. Pound, who held pragmatism up as an ideal and who was rooted in the profession, might have joined Judge Harry Edwards in criticizing the excesses of the movement of legal scholarship toward abstract scholarship (which either has little relevance to concrete issues, or addresses concrete issues in a wholly theoretical manner) and away from scholarship of practical use to the practicing bar and bench.[81]

Pound and his subject, the common law, are examples of the liberal intellectual system. Both are rooted in the intellectual system that grew out of the Enlightenment's conviction that reason, if left free, could discover useful knowledge. This intellectual system is liberal in the sense that it favors individual freedom, open-mindedness, and the use of reason to foster human progress.

The liberal intellectual system is understood as a social community with indefinite possibilities created by human intellectual diversity. The key insight on which the community is based is the recognition of the inherent fallibility of human thought. The bedrock is that any and all of us might, at any time, be wrong. Knowledge is always seen to be tentative and subject to correction. All knowledge claims are revisable. If no person is immune from error, it follows implicitly in the liberal intellectual system that no belief, no matter how strongly held, is above scrutiny for possible correction. No person can claim to be above being checked by others.

The incremental development of the common law, Professors Edgar Bodenhemer and Mary Ann Glendon observe, is a form of dialectical reasoning similar to the scientific method of hypothesis testing. Both approaches are inherent in the liberal intellectual system.

Dialectical reasoning, in Glendon's terms,

> attends to available data and experience, forms hypotheses, tests them against concrete particulars, weighs competing hypotheses, and stands ready to repeat the process in the light of new data, experience, or insight. But unlike the method of the natural sciences, dialectical reasoning begins with premises that are doubtful or

> in dispute. It ends, not with certainty, but with determining which of opposing positions is supported by stronger evidence and more convincing reasons.[82]

Of course dialectical reasoning can never yield the satisfaction of a mathematical proof. It is merely a process by which practical reason and common sense are subject to constant, recursive, reasoned reflection and self scrutiny.[83] Errors are not embedded forever. Over time, the self-correcting processes of dialectical reasoning tend to identify and correct error.

Common law reasoning is a model of dialectical reasoning. Its strength, Pound observed, is a judicial empiricism that combines certainty within reasonable limits with the power of growth in that principles are not fixed authoritatively once and for all, but are discovered and tested gradually through judicial experimentation and experience and the criticism of reported decision by bench and bar.[84]

Pound had bedrock faith in the common law, not as a perfect instrument of law to advance human potential, but as the best doctrine available. He concluded his book, *Spirit of the Common Law*, with these words: "For through all vicissitudes the supremacy of law, the insistence upon law as reason to be developed by judicial experience in the decision of causes, and the refusal to take the burden of upholding right from the concrete case and to put it wholly upon the abstract all have survived."[85] They continue to survive and to serve at the end of the twentieth century as at its beginning.

Pound searched for the spirit of humankind, the keys to human potential, in common law reasoning. He sought a paradigm through which individuals could seek their most enlightened terms of human existence. *The Spirit of the Common Law* guides those who continue the search. The book, and the scholar of profound range who wrote it, embody the best of the liberal intellectual tradition.

NEIL HAMILTON
MATHIAS ALFRED JAREN

NOTES

1. Memorandum from Roscoe Pound to Paul Sayre, his biographer (undated) (on file with the University of Iowa archives, Iowa City, Iowa).

2. Letter from Pound to Sayre (Jan. 8, 1947) (on file with the University of Iowa archives).

3. Letter from Olivia Pound to Sayre (Aug. 2, 1948) (on file with the University of Iowa archives).

4. Paul Sayre, *The Life of Roscoe Pound* (Iowa City: College of Law Committee, State University of Iowa, 1948), 389. Paul Sayre was a law professor at the University of Iowa until 1959. Dean of Iowa Law School William M. Hines remembered Sayre as "One of the most eccentric faculty we've ever had. He always brought his dog to class when lecturing, and on more than one occasion would forget to get off the train when sharing good-

byes with visitors. He would end up in Chicago, no money in his pocket, hours away from Iowa City." Interview with Courtney Jaren, July 1996. In a curious letter to Pound, dated March 18, 1949, a few peculiar phrases can be recounted reinforcing this image of eccentricity: "If you send all the little books together . . . then I will be like an early Christian hermit who has just received some new manuscripts of the gospel story by especial camel delivery at his hut in the desert." (Pound apparently kept scrupulous logs each year of his appointments.) "You speak lightly of your log. It means the life to me as against the mere existence I endure now. . . . [T]hese events alone are enough to start exciting chains of thought in my mind which will lead to all manner of reading of your books and other books, and investigating of other things that will make the final job ten times richer and clearer and truer that it otherwise could be . . . perhaps you overlook my starving condition." Letter from Sayre to Pound (Mar. 18, 1949) (on file with the University of Iowa archives).

5. Dean Arthur Vanderbilt, Address at the Lotus Club, New York (June 28, 1948).

6. Letter from Pound to Sayre (Dec. 1, 1941) (on file with the University of Iowa archives).

7. Letter from Pound to Omer Hershey (Feb. 10, 1895) (on file with the University of Iowa archives); also in Sayre, *The Life of Roscoe Pound*, 85. (Hershey, a Harvard Law classmate and a close friend of Pound's, was in the chocolate business.)

8. See John Chipman Gray, "Methods of Legal Education" (pt. 4), *Yale Law Journal* 1 (1892): 159–161; John Chipman Gray, "Some Definitions and Principles of Jurisprudence," *Harvard Law Review* 6 (1892): 21.

9. Letter from John Chipman Gray to Charles W. Eliot, President of Harvard (Jan. 8, 1883), in Mark Dewolfe Howe, *Justice Oliver Wendell Holmes: The Proving Years, 1870–1882* (Cambridge, Mass.: Belknap Press, 1963), 158.

10. David Wigdor, *Roscoe Pound, Philosopher of Law* (Westport, Conn.: Greenwood Press, 1974), 35.

11. Letter from Holmes to Pollock (July 6, 1908) in Mark DeWolfe Howe, ed., *Holmes-Pollock Letters: The Correspondence of Mr. Justice Holmes and Sir Frederick Pollock, 1874–1932,* 2nd ed. (Cambridge, Mass.: Belknap Press, 1961), 140.

12. Letter from Oliver Wendell Holmes, Jr., to Sir Frederick Pollock (Apr. 10, 1881) in Howe, *Holmes-Pollock Letters*, 17.

13. Bryan, later to become a presidential hopeful, was an orator of the "Chataqua Circuit" and an opponent against Clarence Darrow (who Pound would meet in Chicago, in the next decade) in the infamous 1925 Scopes Trial. It is notable to observe the connections between lawyers who would later become national figures.

14. *Green Bag* 8 (1896): 172, 173. (According to the editors of this periodical, "An Entertaining Magazine for Lawyers.")

15. Ibid., 172.

16. *Williams v. Miles*, 68 Neb. 463, 470; 94 N.W. 705, 708 (1903). This is a prophetic observation which runs strongly in Pound's articles.

17. Roscoe Pound, "The Decadence of Equity," *Columbia Law Review* 5 (1905): 20. As with many of his writings, Pound had already made a speech to some association, in this case, the materials for the "Decadence of Equity" were

presented to the Nebraska Bar Association's third annual meeting. Because of that meeting, Pound would be solicited by the president of the ABA to present the next year at St. Paul, which, in turn, resulted in Wigmore of Northwestern recruiting Pound to Northwestern as professor of law.

18. Albert Kocourek, "Roscoe Pound as a Former Colleague Knew Him," in Paul Sayre, ed., *Interpretations of Modern Legal Philosophies: Essays in Honor of Roscoe Pound* (New York: Oxford University Press, 1947), 419.

19. Paul Sayre, "Introduction," in Sayre, *Interpretations of Modern Legal Philosophies*, 3–13.

20. Thomas A. Cowan, "Legal Pragmatism and Beyond," in Sayre, *Interpretations of Modern Legal Philosophies*, 14, 130.

21. Wigdor, *Roscoe Pound*, x.

22. Looking back upon his earlier work, Pound, ever the pragmatist, tells Sayre: "What has given me pause is that a number of things which I have written need to be revised or rewritten, and some others I should like to use, at least in large part, in the book on Jurisprudence which I still hope to be able to finish...." Letter from Pound to Sayre (Dec. 11, 1943) (on file with the University of Iowa archives).

23. See Kocourek, "Roscoe Pound," 419–420 (quoting letter from Holmes to Pollock [Mar. 10, 1923] in Howe, *Holmes-Pollock Letters*, 115).

24. Pound, "Decadence," 28.

25. Ibid., 20.

26. Ibid., 24.

27. Roscoe Pound, "Do We Need a Philosophy of Law?," *Columbia Law Review* 5 (1905): 339.

28. Ibid., 344.

29. *Lochner v. New York*, 198 U.S. 45 (1905).

30. *Muller v. Oregon*, 208 U.S. 412 (1908).

31. Pound, "Do We Need a Philosophy of Law?," 345.

32. Ibid., 346.

33. Ibid., 349.

34. Ibid., 351.

35. Ibid., (quoting *Loan Association v. Topeka*, 87 U.S. [20 Wall.] 655 [1874]).

36. Ibid., 352.

37. *Green Bag* 18 (1906): 17.

38. Ibid., 17.

39. Ibid., 18.

40. Ibid., 22.

41. Ibid., 24.

42. See Roscoe Pound, "The Causes of Popular Dissatisfaction with the Administration of Justice," in *ABA Reports* 29 (1906): 395–417.

43. Wigmore was already dean of Northwestern University School of Law.

44. John H. Wigmore, "Roscoe Pound's St. Paul Address of 1906: The Spark That Kindled the White Flame of Progress," *Journal of American Judicature Society* 20 (1937): 176.

45. Ibid., 178. "Just thirty years ago last August was struck the spark that kindled the white flame of high endeavor, now spreading through the entire legal profession and radiating the spirit of resolute progress in the administration of justice. Until that spark was struck, the profession was a complacent self-satisfied, genial fellowship of individual lawyers—unalive to the shortcomings of our justice, unthinking of the urgent demands of the impending future, unconscious of their potential opportunities, unaware of their collective duty and destiny," 176.

46. Roscoe Pound, "Executive Justice," *American Law Register* 46 (1907): 137. This journal became the *University of Pennsylvania Law Review.*

47. Ibid., 139.

48. Ibid.

49. Ibid., 140.

50. Ibid., 144–45.

51. Ibid., 145.

52. Ibid., 146.

53. Roscoe Pound, "Spurious Interpretations," *Columbia Law Review* 7 (1907): 379.

54. See John Austin, "Essays on Interpretation and Analogy," in Robert Campbell, ed., *Austin's Jurisprudence*, 5th ed. (London: J. Murray, 1885), 989.

55. Pound, "Spurious Interpretations," 381.

56. Ibid., 385.

57. Ibid., 386. The words echo Professor Sheldon Amos: "Government, again, is the most restless of all institutions, and the most intractable under the yoke of custom, and so far as its activity or its forms are regulated by traditional usage, the validity and integrity of those forms are being constantly exposed to the most searching and public test," Sheldon Amos, *Science of Law* (London: H. S. King, 1877), 50. Amos too argued that,

> The main machinery for the conversion of desultory and uncertain customs into fixed rules, needing only the complete development of Government to transmute them into true law, are the decisions which are constantly demanded for the purpose of ascertaining, for a practical purpose, the true purport and extent of an alleged custom. . . . If the community progresses, the law must needs expand

and become a more and more exact expression of the moral sensibilities and economical habits of the people.

This expansion can only be effected in two ways—that of direct legislation, proceeding from the supreme political authority, and that of indirect legislation, proceeding from the judges who are called upon to execute the law. As to the former way, that of direct legislation, the meaning and method of it are sufficiently understood in the present day, when it is the main and, apparently, the most natural method of introducing changes of the law. But the large mass of the law of every civilized country has been developed in the process of executing law, though a variety of different methods have been consciously or unconsciously employed for this purpose.

The legislator must needs put the general tendency and consequences of a law in a higher rank of importance than its occasional operation. If, on the whole, the law seems likely to promote a balance of good over evil, for him the law is a good one and should be retained or introduced.

The judge, on the other hand, having a vast number of laws to execute, some of them only on very few occasions, is more arrested by the special operation of a law in the particular instances which come before him, than by the general consequences of the law which he is less bound to think about. The special operation of a law he can inspect with a distinctness which no legislator, contemplating the circumstances of men's personal history and the accidents of human life only at a distance, can rival. (Pp. 53–54)

Pound's writing incorporates many of Amos' earlier themes.

58. Roscoe Pound, "The Need of a Sociological Jurisprudence," *Green Bag* 19 (1907): 607.

59. See Amos, *Science of Law*, 55: "The practice of legal fictions, by which the imaginative reverence for old symbols and formalities is deferred to while more or less perceptible change is introduced into the substance of the law, is now thoroughly understood, and has been fully commented upon. Sometimes, by the medium of a fiction the legislature itself is imposed upon, and is lulled into acquiescence with a policy which, when distinctly presented to it, it would disown, or has actually disowned."

60. Pound, "Spurious Interpretations," 607.

61. Ibid., 607–608.

62. Ibid., 611.

63. Ibid., 612.

64. Ibid.

65. Roscoe Pound, "The Scope and Purpose of Sociological Jurisprudence," *Harvard Law Review* 24 (1911): 591.

66. Ibid., 597.

67. Roscoe Pound, "Theories of Law," *Yale Law Journal* 22 (1912): 114, 143.

68. Roscoe Pound, "The Administration of Justice in the Modern City," *Harvard Law Review* 26 (1913): 302, 324.

69. Ibid., 309.

70. Ibid., 327.

71. Roscoe Pound, *The Spirit of the Common Law* (New Brunswick, NJ: Transaction Publishers, 1998; Boston: Beacon Press, 1921), 182–83.

72. Ibid., 182.

73. Ibid., 89–90.

74. See ibid., 13, 64, 101, and 111.

75. See ibid., xii, 6–7.

76. Ibid., 98–99.

77. Ibid., xii, 6–7.

78. Ibid., 73.

79. See ibid., 189–90.

80. Ibid., 181.

81. See Harry T. Edwards, "The Growing Distinction Between Legal Education and the Legal Profession," *Michigan Law Review* 91 (1992): 34.

82. Mary Ann Glendon, *A Nation Under Lawyers* (New York: Farrar, Straus and Giroux, 1994), 238.

83. Ibid.

84. Pound, *Spirit of the Common Law*, 181–183. As a defender of the Enlightenment, Pound was one of the 15 members of the American Association of University Professors' first Committee on Academic Freedom and Tenure. The committee drafted the AAUP's 1915 Declaration of Principles, the most important document defining the American concept of academic freedom.

85. Ibid., 216.

PREFACE TO THE 1963 EDITION

NO living man has exercised so profound an influence on legal thought as Dean Pound. At ninety-three he is a living legend whose fame is world wide. He published his first article in 1896 and still writes on many topics and invariably with pervasive insight. One may agree or disagree with his always provocative comments on any given subject—that is not important—one always learns something from his writings and that is terribly important. A 1960 bibliography of his books and articles totalled over a thousand published items. No man of the law has approached Dean Pound's extraordinary contribution to legal literature.

The Spirit of the Common Law is one of Dean Pound's most notable works. It contains the brilliant lectures he delivered at Dartmouth College in the summer of 1921. It is a seminal book embodying the spiritual essence of sociological jurisprudence by its leading prophet.

The Spirit of the Common Law had a wide vogue among lawyers and laymen alike when first published. It deserves a wide vogue now. It is a sprightly book concerning law, not musty trade tool for lawyers. It reaches to the wide audience seeking an understandable picture of our legal institutions. It is brief, and yet comprehensive; scholarly, but with a light touch.

I remember well my first reading of the book as a freshman law student in 1926. My fellows and I were excited and attracted by the new judicial philosophy expounded by the author. He called for an infusion of social ideals into the traditional elements of the law; he insisted that consideration of the public weal, as well as of private interests, must play a part in the law's development, and he demanded that the law change to keep abreast of new social conditions.

Virtually two generations of American judges and lawyers have responded, and our law today is different in a very real sense because of this and other books and writings of Dean Pound.

In rereading the book now, I am particularly impressed with the admirable chapter "Puritanism and the Law" and "The Pioneers and the Law." They provide remarkable insights into the influence of the Puritan and the Pioneer on our present legal institutions. Both have indelibly stamped on our law an insistence upon a maximum of individual liberty and resistance to authoritarian government.

The Puritans and the Pioneers carried this resistance to extremes. They came to oppose necessary legislative change and essential reforms in law and in procedure, but, nevertheless, left us a precious heritage of respect for the dignity and rights of the individual.

Dean Pound correctly forecast in this book almost a half-century ago the imperative necessity of reconciling social and individual interests—a process in which we are still engaged.

The Spirit of the Common Law will always be treasured by judges and lawyers for its philosophy and history, but more importantly for Dean Pound's optimism and faith in the capacity of law to keep up with the times without sacrificing fundamental values. It is a faith built upon the conviction that the present is not to be divorced from the past, but rather that the past and the present are to be built upon to make a better future.

ARTHUR J. GOLDBERG
The Supreme Court of the United States
May 1, 1963

FOREWORD TO THE 1921 EDITION

THE Dartmouth Alumni Lectureships have been established upon the theory that the influence of the intellectual life of the College ought to be available, in some degree at least, to others than those who are in residence as students,—as for example, to graduates who are solicitous for some contact with the College which will help to maintain the breadth of their scholarship; or to friends who are interested in the kinds of intellectual interest for which the College wishes to stand.

The suggestion of the particular form which the project of these lectureships has taken was made in my inaugural address in 1916 when statement was made as follows:

"I am very sure that the contribution of the College to its graduates ought to be continued in some more tangible way than exists at present. The tendency of college men to seek careers outside the professions, the tendencies of the professions themselves to become so highly specialized as to necessitate the complete engrossment of thought of the men who follow them, and the ever increasing demand of the age on all, requiring constantly greater intensity of effort and more exclusive utilization of time in men who wish to do their respective shares of the world's work, impose a duty upon the college which formerly belonged to it in no such degree, if at all. Contacts with what we broadly classify as the arts and sciences are less and less possible for men of affairs. In many a graduate the interest in or enthusiasm for these which the college arouses is, therefore, altogether likely to languish, or even die, for lack of sustenance. If the College, then, has conviction that its influence is worth seeking at the expense of four vital years in the formative period of life, is it not logically compelled to search for some method of giving access to this influence to its graduates in their subsequent years! The growing practice of retiring men from active work at ages from sixty-five to seventy, and the not infrequent tragedy of the man who has no resources for interesting himself outside the routine of which he has been relieved, make it seem that the College has no less an opportunity to be of service to its men in their old age than in their youth, if only it can establish the procedure by which it can periodically throughout their lives give them opportunity to replenish their intellectual reserves. It is possible that something in the way of courses of lectures by certain recognized leaders of the world's thought, made available for alumni and friends of the College during a brief period immediately following the Commencement season, would be a step in this direction. Or it may be that some other device would more completely realize the possibilities. It at least seems clear that the formal educational contacts between the College and its graduates should not stop at the end of four years, never in any form to be renewed."

The carrying out of the plan, with such purpose in view, was made possible by the hearty endorsement of Mr. Henry Lynn Moore of the class of 1877—and a Trustee of Dartmouth College—and by his promise of generous financial assistance to establish in this form a memorial, to keep alive the memory of his beloved son, Guernsey Center Moore, of the class of 1904, who died early in his college course.

The completion of the plans for the lectureships was originally set for an earlier time, but the World War interrupted. It was, therefore, not until the summer of 1921 that the experiment was finally undertaken with Professor Roscoe Pound, the brilliant and scholarly Dean of Harvard Law School, and Mr. Ralph Adams Cram, noted architect and original thinker, as lecturers upon this Foundation.

It has, of course, been recognized from the beginning that the extension of the influence of these lectures would be largely increased by publication, which should make the mental stimulation in them available to wider groups than, under any circumstances, could be expected to be in attendance as auditors during any course. It is, therefore, with much satisfaction that there is presented herewith the lectures of Dean Pound for the consideration, on the one hand, of the considerable group who heard him and have since been desirous of the lectures in printed form as well as, on the other hand, that far greater constituency to whom attendance was not possible to hear the spoken word, but whose interest in the speaker and the subject has been keen. To all of these this book on "The Spirit of the Common Law" from the hands of Dean Pound will be of major interest.

ERNEST MARTIN HOPKINS

PREFACE TO THE 1921 EDITION

IN 1914 I gave a course at the Lowell Institute upon this same subject, summaries of which, based upon reports of the lectures in the Boston Transcript, were published in the Green Bag (vol. 26, p. 166). Also the first lecture of that course was published in the International Journal of Ethics (vol. 25, p. 1). In 1910 I delivered an address before the Kansas State Bar Association upon the subject of the second lecture, which was published in the proceedings of that Association (Proc., 1910, p. 45) and reprinted in the American Law Review (vol. 45, p. 811). An address on the subject of the third lecture was delivered before the Iowa State Bar Association in 1914 and is published in its proceedings (vol. 20, p. 96). It was also delivered before the Worcester County (Mass.) Bar Association which printed it for private circulation. An address on the subject of the fifth lecture was delivered before the Bar Association of North Carolina in 1920 and published in the proceedings of that year. This address was reprinted in the West Virginia Law Quarterly (vol. 27, p. 1). All these materials have been used freely, but all have been revised and much has been wholly rewritten.

As these lectures speak in large part from the second decade of the present century, they show the faith in the efficacy of effort and belief that the administration of justice may be improved by conscious intelligent action which characterized that time. The recrudescence of juristic pessimism in the past three years has not led me to abandon that point of view. At the end of the nineteenth century lawyers thought attempt at conscious improvement was futile. Now many of them think it is dangerous. In the same way the complacent nothing-needs-to-be-done attitude of Blackstone, who in the spirit of the end of a period of growth thought the law little short of a state of perfection, was followed by the timorous juristic pessimism of Lord Eldon who feared that law reform would subvert the constitution. Not a little in the legislative reform movement which followed might have proceeded on more conservative lines if he had been willing to further needed changes instead of obstructing all change. The real danger to administration of justice according to law is in timid resistance to rational improvement and obstinate persistence in legal paths which have become impossible in the heterogeneous, urban, industrial America of today. Such things have been driving us fast to an administrative justice through boards and commissions, with loosely defined powers, unlimited discretion and inadequate judicial restraints, which is at variance with the genius of our legal and political institutions.

Nor were the efforts of the decades of faith in progress as futile as it is fashionable for the moment to think them. Sometimes, as in projects for recall, they displayed more zeal than intelligent understanding of the task. But who would do away with the Municipal Court of Chicago and the modern city Courts which have arisen in its image? Who would wipe out the simplifications of practice which were brought about after 1900 at the instance of bar associations? Who would return to the condition of industrial accident litigation at the end of the nineteenth century, or revive the state of things in which every act of administration encountered an injunction, or restore the attitude of the bench from 1890 to 1910 when, in many state courts, any statute which went upon unfamiliar premises or departed from historical lines was *prima facie* unconstitutional.

When eighteenth-century common-law pleading had become impossible in nineteenth-century America, one of the great lawyers of the time was called upon to serve upon the commission which framed the first code of civil procedure. Had he been willing to put his skill and knowledge to the work of rational improvement, legal procedure in the majority of our states might be far different from what it is, and the conflict between legislative endeavor to reform and judicial refusal to walk in new paths, which has marked the history of "code pleading," might have been averted. Moreover, had the judges of the first half of the century possessed sufficient vision to exercise their common-law powers and had they done even some part of what Chief Justice Doe did in New Hampshire, it is not unlikely that the movement for an elective bench which swept over the country about 1850, putting the courts into politics and seriously impairing the judicial independence which is vital in our law, might have proceeded more slowly, have extended to relatively few frontier communities and have spared the higher tribunals. When the lawyer refuses to act intelligently, unintelligent application of the legislative steam-roller by the layman is the alternative.

ROSCOE POUND
Harvard Law School
August 5, 1921

THE SPIRIT OF THE COMMON LAW

I

THE FEUDAL ELEMENT

PERHAPS no institution of the modern world shows such vitality and tenacity as our Anglo-American legal tradition which we call the common law. Although it is essentially a mode of judicial and juristic thinking, a mode of treating legal problems rather than a fixed body of definite rules, it succeeds everywhere in molding rules, whatever their origin, into accord with its principles and in maintaining those principles in the face of formidable attempts to overthrow or to supersede them. In the United States it survives the huge mass of legislation that is placed annually upon our statute books and gives to it form and consistency. Nor is it less effective in competition with law of foreign origin. Louisiana alone of the states carved from the Louisiana purchase preserves the French law. In Texas only a few anomalies in procedure serve to remind us that another system once prevailed in that domain. In California only the institution of community property remains to tell us that the Spanish law once obtained in that jurisdiction. Only historians know that the custom of Paris once governed in Michigan and Wisconsin. And in Louisiana not only is the criminal law wholly English, but the fundamental common-law institutions, supremacy of law, case law and hearing of causes as a whole in open court, have imposed themselves on a French code and have made great portions of the law Anglo-American in all but name. There are many signs that the common law is imposing itself gradually in like manner upon the French law in Quebec. In everything but terminology it has all but overcome a received Roman law in Scotland. The established Roman-Dutch law in South Africa is slowly giving way before it as the judges more and more reason in a Romanized terminology after the manner of common-law lawyers. In the Philippines and in Porto Rico there are many signs that common-law administration of a Roman code will result in a system Anglo-American in substance if Roman-Spanish in its terms.

Whether it is the innate excellence of our legal system or the innate cocksureness of the people that live under it, so that even as Mr. Podsnap talked to the Frenchman as if he were a deaf child, we assume that our common-law notions are part of the legal order of nature and are unable to understand that any reasonable being can harbor legal conceptions that run counter to them, the Anglo-Saxon refuses to be ruled by any other law. Even more, he succeeds in ruling others thereby. For the strength of the common law is in its treatment of concrete controversies, as the strength of its rival, the modern Roman law, is in its logical development of abstract conceptions. Hence wherever the administration of justice is mediately or immediately in the hands of common-law judges their habit of applying to the cause in hand the judicial experience of the past rather than attempting to fit the cause into its exact logical pigeonhole in an abstract system gradually undermines the competing body of law and makes for a slow but persistent invasion of the common law.

At but one point has our Anglo-American legal tradition met with defeat in its competition with the rival tradition. The contest of French law, English law and German law, in the framing of the new codes for Japan, was won decisively by the German law. And yet this was not a contest of English with German law. It was a competition between systems of legal rules, not between modes of judicial administration of justice. In a comparison of abstract systems the common law is at its worst. In a test of the actual handling of single controversies it has always prevailed. Nor is this all. The American development of the common-law doctrine of supremacy of law, in our characteristic institution of judicial power over unconstitutional legislation, is commending itself to peoples who have to administer written federal constitutions. In the reports of South American republics we find judicial discussions of constitutional problems fortified with citation of American authorities. In the South African reports we find a court composed of Dutch judges, trained in the Roman-Dutch law, holding a legislative act invalid and citing *Marbury* v. *Madison*—the foundation of American constitutional law—along with the modern civilians.

The Australian bench and bar, notwithstanding a decision of the judicial committee of the Privy Council in England, are insisting upon the authority of Australian courts to pass upon the constitutionality of state statutes; and the Privy Council has found itself obliged to pronounce invalid a confiscatory statute enacted by a Canadian province. Even Continental publicists may be found asserting it a fundamental defect of their public law that constitutional principles are not protected by an independent court of justice. Moreover, if in the eighteenth century, while the absorption of the law merchant was in progress, Anglo-American law received not a little of the civil law indirectly, through the Continental treatises on commercial law which exercised so wide an influence at that time, in the nineteenth century we were well avenged. In the more recent development of the subject the commercial law evolved in the English courts has played a leading part, and Continental jurists do not hesitate to admit that in this way a considerable measure of English law has been received into European legal systems. When we add that the most significant movement today in the countries that received the Roman law is a change of front from the Byzantine idea of a closed system of rules, authoritatively laid down, which judges may only apply in a mechanical fashion, in the direction of the common-law idea of judicial law-making through the decision of causes, it must be conceded that our Anglo-American system, no less than its older rival, is a law of the world.

Vitality and tenacity are not new qualities in our

legal tradition. It has been able to receive and to absorb the most diverse bodies of doctrine and the most divergent bodies of rules, developed outside of itself, without disturbing its essential unity. Equity, the law as to misdemeanors made in the Star Chamber, the law merchant, admiralty, the law as to probate and divorce made in the ecclesiastical courts, and the statutes of the nineteenth-century legislative reform movement in England and the United States, have been, as it were, digested and assimilated. For although we are wont to say of some of these that they made over the common law, it is quite as true that the common law made them over. In each case their alien characters have steadily disappeared and today they show few points of difference from the institutions and doctrines of pure common-law pedigree by which they are surrounded.

Moreover, the common law has passed triumphantly through more than one crisis in which it seemed that an alien system might supersede it; it has contended with more than one powerful antagonist and has come forth victor. In the twelfth century it strove for jurisdiction with the church, the strongest force of that time. In the sixteenth century, when the Roman law was sweeping over Europe and superseding the endemic law on every hand, the common law stood firm. Neither the three R's, as Maitland calls them, Renaissance, Reformation, and Reception of Roman law, nor the partial reversion to justice without law under the Tudors shook the hold of our legal tradition. In the seventeenth century it contended with the English crown and established its doctrine of the supremacy of law against the Stuart kings. In America, after the Revolution, it prevailed over the prejudice against all things English, which for a time threatened a reception of French law, developed its doctrine of the supremacy of law to its ultimate logical conclusion in the teeth of the strongest political influence of the time, and maintained its doctrine of precedent, involving the unpopular practice of citing English decisions, in spite of the hostility to lawyers and to systematic legal administration of justice characteristic of new communities. It is not too much to say that the common law passed through these several crises with its distinctive fundamental ideas not merely unshaken but more firmly settled.

Superficially, then, the triumph of the common law and its establishment as a law of the world by the side of the Roman law, seem secure. And yet at the very moment of triumph it is evident that a new crisis is at hand. If not actually upon trial in the United States, the common law is certainly under indictment. If we look at the three most striking examples of its present world-wide extension—its doctrine of the supremacy of law, its commercial law and its law of torts—its doctrine of supremacy of law and consequent judicial power over unconstitutional legislation is bitterly attacked in the land of its origin and is endangering the independence and authority of the court which is the central point of the Anglo-American system; its commercial law is codifying in England and in America; and in its law of torts the sentence of death which hangs over contributory negligence, assumption of risk and the doctrine that liability may flow only from fault appears to many of its votaries to involve characteristic principles of the whole system. It is true the world-wide movement for socialization of law, the shifting from the abstract individualist justice of the past century to a newer ideal of justice, as yet none too clearly perceived, is putting a strain upon all law everywhere. In the United States, however, there is more than this. Here, beyond this strain which is felt wherever law obtains, the rise of executive justice, the tendency to commit everything to boards and commissions which proceed extrajudicially and are expected to be law unto themselves, the breakdown of our polity of individual initiative in the enforcement of law and substitution of administrative inspection and supervision, and the failure of the popular feeling for justice at all events which the common law postulates appear to threaten a complete change in our attitude toward legal problems.

Nor is our law well-prepared in all respects to meet the present crisis. The conditions of judicial lawmaking in the United States are by no means those which are demanded for the best development of the common law in an era of growth. The institution of an elective judiciary, holding for short terms, which prevails in so many of our jurisdictions, does not give us courts adequate to such a task. Indeed, the illiberal decisions of which complaint was made so widely at the beginning of the twentieth century were largely, one might say almost wholly, the work of popularly-elected judges. A system of lawmaking through judicial empiricism calls for much more in a judge than popularity, honest mediocrity or ignorant zeal for the public welfare may insure. In the period of growth in the fore part of the last century there was a strong, independent bench. That American law grew so rapidly and was fashioned so well up to the Civil War and stood still so steadfastly thereafter, was by no means wholly due to causes of general operation that made for rigidity of law throughout the world in the nineteenth century. It is demonstrable that this change was due in large measure to a change in the character of the bench in our state courts, closely connected with the change in the mode of choice and tenure of judges which swept over the country after 1850. Moreover, the condition of pressure under which causes are passed upon in the American urban communities of today, where crowded calendars preclude the thoroughness in presentation and deliberation in judicial study which were possible a century ago, prevent judicial lawmaking from achieving its best. An example from the law reports will make clear what this means. In 4 Wheaton's Reports, reporting the decisions of the Supreme Court of the United States during the year 1819, decisions in thirty-three cases are reported. In other words, seven judges decided thirty-three cases in that year. In 248-251 United States Reports, we may see the work of that court a hundred years later. In 1919 the court wrote two hundred and forty-two opinions and disposed of six hundred and sixty-one cases. If we look only at the opinions written, where seven judges wrote thirty-three opinions in 1819, nine judges wrote two hundred and forty-two opinions in 1919. In other words, merely in the way of writing opinions, a judge of that court does five times what he had to do a century ago. This does not mean merely that the judges are compelled to work rapidly and with a minimum of deliberation. In order to hear these cases at all the time allowed to counsel must be greatly abridged. Hence where a century ago counsel were heard until every detail had been gone into thoroughly in oral argument, today the court is compelled to restrict argument to an allowance of an hour and a half to counsel upon each side. In state courts the pressure has become even greater. Thus at a time when constructive work of the highest order is demanded, when questions are raising more difficult than any with which American judges had to deal in our classical constructive period—the period from the Revolution to the Civil War—in many of our states the courts are none too well equipped to do the work effectively and in all of them the pressure of business is such that work of the highest type is all but precluded.

Perceiving the condition rather than the causes of unsatisfactory judicial administration of justice men have been coming forward with all manner of supposed cures. Perhaps the most popular is to tinker the judicial organization, carrying still further the tearing down of the Anglo-American judicial office and the subjection of the judge to politics. Another is to supersede the common law by a mass of detailed legislation which aims to leave nothing to the judge.

Another goes to the opposite extreme and urges that we abandon all juristic premises and put judicial lawmaking at large as completely as legislative lawmaking. The lawyer ought not to sit by silently when such proposals, flying in the face of all that experience has taught us in the course of legal history, are making head in the community. That they sometimes have gained adherents among the thoughtful and patriotic in the immediate past makes it timely for him to examine the body of legal tradition on which he relies, to ascertain the elements of which it is made up, to learn its spirit, and to perceive how it has come to be what it is, to the end that we may know how far we may make use of it in the stage of legal development upon which the world has now entered.

No doubt there are those who will think the lawyer must apologize, or at least must show cause, for all but the last of these inquiries. For it may be conceded that historical jurisprudence, for the moment, is discredited. The fashion of the time calls for a sociological legal history; for a study not merely of how legal doctrines have evolved and developed considered only as jural materials, but of the social causes and social effects of doctrines and of the relations of legal history to social and economic history. I should be the last to deny the great importance of this feature of the program of the sociological jurist. But it is possible to overrate the value of this type of legal history for juristic purposes. Just as a past generation, seeing rightly that there was an intimate connection between law and politics, assumed that the political interpretation of jurisprudence and legal history was the whole story, so another generation, seeing rightly that there is an intimate relation between law and economics, may make the same assumption of all-sufficiency for the economic interpretation of jurisprudence and legal history, and that without much more warrant. For by and large the economic interpretation of legal history has been sustained by examples drawn from legislation which has failed to leave any permanent mark in the law or by a superficial view of particular juristic or judicial doctrines out of their true juridical setting. In truth two powerful forces have counteracted economic pressure and class interest throughout the history of law, and have prevented the law of peoples that have attained any degree of legal development from being what economic forces or class conflict might else have made it. These are, first, the insistence upon development of law logically from analogies of existing rules and doctrines, both because it was supposed the jurist or the judge could not make law but could only find it and because the demand for certainty and predicability, resting on the social interest in security, was held to require him to deduce according to a known technique from premises already existing, and, second, conscious endeavor to make law express supposed eternal and unchangeable ideals.

Conscious, constructive lawmaking is a late phenomenon in legal history. In primitive society the idea of sacred law or of settled custom, all departure wherefrom is dangerous, in a later stage the authority of fixed ascertainments of the traditional law, and later still the conception of an eternal and immutable natural law, of which the law of the time and place is but declaratory—all these make against conscious and deliberate creation of law by the free setting up of new premises or by the promulgation of rules which cannot be derived or made to appear derived from existing premises. Even in periods of growth, in which ideals are sought avowedly and attempt is made to shape the law thereto, an identification of these ideals with an ideal development of received legal principles is not unlikely to be the outcome. This tendency to rational working out of the jural materials in the traditional system and the demand for certainty lead jurists and judges to resort to analogy whenever they are confronted with a new problem. They fortify what would be, no doubt, a natural tendency so to proceed in any event. Hence the chiefest factor in determining the course which legal development will take with respect to any new situation or new problem is the analogy or analogies that chance to be at hand when those whose function it is to lay down the law are called upon to make an authoritative determination.

Legal history, then, may be made to show us the analogies, the legal premises, which have developed as the potential bases of legal growth. It may be made to show us the ideals which have developed, to which jurists and judges have sought to make law conform by logical use of these analogies and logical drawing out of these premises. It may be made to show the way in which the working out of these analogies and the logical development of these premises have determined both the content and the spirit of the tradition which is the most important part of our law both in bulk and in intrinsic significance. It may be admitted that this is not all we shall need in order to make effort effective in achieving the purposes of law in a new period of growth. But it is a large part and an essential part. For the inquiry will be nothing less than a taking stock of the materials with which we must work, since, in the long run, the condition of law depends upon the condition of the traditional element in the legal system, by which legislative rules are interpreted and developed and into which, if they succeed in establishing themselves as law, enacted rules are absorbed and incorporated.

If we look narrowly at our legal tradition we shall see that it has two characteristics. On the one hand, it is characterized by an extreme individualism. A foreign observer has said that its distinguishing marks are "unlimited valuation of individual liberty and respect for individual property." It is concerned not with social righteousness but with individual rights. It tries questions of the highest social import as mere private controversies between John Doe and Richard Roe. Its respect for the individual makes procedure, civil and criminal, ultra-contentious, and preserves in the modern world the archaic theory of litigation as a fair fight, according to the canons of the manly art, with a court to see fair play and prevent interference. Moreover it is so zealous to secure fair play to the individual that often it secures very little fair play to the public. It relies on individual initiative to enforce the law and vindicate the right. It is jealous of all interference with individual freedom of action, physical, mental, or economic. In short, the isolated individual is the center of many of its most significant doctrines. On the other hand, it is characterized by another element tending in quite another direction; a tendency to affix duties and liabilities independently of the will of those bound, to look to relations rather than to legal transactions as the basis of legal consequences, and to impose both liabilities and disabilities upon those standing in certain relations as members of a class rather than upon individuals.

What has determined these characteristics of our legal tradition? How does it come to be so thoroughly, so obstinately individualist in a time that looks more and more to social control for a solution of its problems and is bringing about a socialization of pretty much everything except the common law? How does it come that at the same time this tradition contains another element of an opposite tendency, an element that leads it to deal with men in groups or classes or relations and not as individuals? These questions demand our attention before we assume to pronounce what we may make of our traditional jural materials for the purposes of today and of tomorrow.

Seven factors of the first importance appear to have contributed to shape our American common law. These are: (1) An original substratum of Germanic legal institutions and jural ideas; (2) the feudal law; (3) Puritanism; (4) the contests between the courts and the crown in the seventeenth century; (5) eighteenth-century political ideas; (6) the conditions of pioneer or agricultural communities in America in the first half of the nineteenth century, and (7) the philosophical ideas with respect to justice, law and the state that prevailed in the formative period in which the English common law was made over for us by American courts. All but one of these made strongly for individualism, and it is to them that we must trace the intense individualism that made the classical common-law tradition so out of accord with popular feeling in the first decade of the present century. One of them, however, namely the feudal law, has given to our legal system a fundamental mode of thought, a mode of dealing with legal situations and with legal problems which gives wholly different results, a mode of thought which has always tempered the individualism of our law, and now that the change from a pioneer, agricultural, rural society to a settled, industrial and commercial and even predominantly urban society calls for a new order of legal ideas, has been the chief resource of the courts in the movement which has long been proceeding quietly beneath the surface in judicial decision. Let us remember that the high-water mark of individualism in American law was reached in the last quarter of the nineteenth century. Before that signs of a reaction were appearing, and the common-law tradition proved to have in itself a principle which could be employed to carry forward that reaction without any general disturbance of the legal system.

In considering the foregoing factors in order and in appraising the extent to which and the manner in which they have influenced or fashioned the common law, a few words as to the substratum of Germanic law will suffice.

Speaking broadly, it is true that for all but academic purposes the history of English law begins in the thirteenth century. Yet it is equally true that no arbitrary beginning may be assigned to any institution. In law especially, where until modern times conscious making of much that was new was quite unthinkable, nothing is made at once, as it were, out of whole cloth. There were few anywhere who knew any too much of Roman law when the system that grew up in the courts of the Norman kings had its beginnings, and certainly what was known of it in England was superficial enough. The materials with which the first common-law judges wrought were Germanic materials. The ideas from which and with which they laid the foundations of the Anglo-American legal system were ideas of Germanic law. So thoroughly did they lay them, so great was the advantage to the law of strong, central courts of justice administering the king's law for the whole realm as the common law thereof, that our law is today more Germanic than the law of Germany itself. The Norman conquest brought a Romance element into our speech. But it brought relatively little that was Roman into the law. When later the Roman law swept over Continental Europe, the traditional law, local, provincial, and conflicting on the Continent, was general, unified, and harmonious in England. In England, therefore, with a vigorous, central judicial system behind it and an established course of teaching in the Inns of Court which gave it the toughness of a taught tradition, the Germanic law persisted. When in the seventeenth century the labors of Coke gave it the form in which we received it in America, the common law was an English development of Germanic legal ideas. Roman law undoubtedly contributed many analogies and many conceptions which were worked into the system. But they were worked over as well as worked in and acquired the character of endemic law. Accordingly because of the attempt at Germanization of the law of the German empire as a result of the Germanist movement in the nineteenth century and the substitution of Germanic doctrines for Roman here and there in the new civil code, our law has in it less of the Roman than the Romanized law of Germany has of the Germanic.

That the substratum of our law is Germanic is something of much more than academic interest. It means that the basis of American law, the material out of which American judges in the nineteenth century made the law under which we live, represents the stage of legal development which may be called the stage of the strict law. On the other hand, the basis of the common law of Continental Europe, the Digest of Justinian, made up of extracts from the writings of the classical Roman jurists, represents the later stage of legal development which may be called the stage of equity or natural law. Our law also went through that later stage. But in the maturity of our law we still had a double system in which each stage of legal development was represented. In Continental Europe, on the contrary, the materials on which legal development proceeded after the reception of Roman law, had been all but purged of the characteristic features of the stage of the strict law before they were handed down to the modern world. In consequence our judicial tradition, speaking from our classical period, the period in which Coke and his contemporaries summed up and restated the law developed by English courts from the thirteenth to the fifteenth century, in a sense speaks from the stage of the strict law. The Continental juristic tradition, speaking from the Byzantine version of the classical Roman jurists, who wrote from the first to the third century, and representing, not the strict, archaic *ius ciuile* but the liberal, modern *ius gentium* and *ius naturale,* speaks from the stage of equity or natural law.

Individualism is a prime characteristic of the stage of legal development to which I have referred as the strict law. For example, the strict law insists upon full and exact performance at all events of a duty undertaken in legal form. It makes no allowance for accident and has no mercy for defaulters. When a debtor in the sixteenth century incurred a heavy forfeiture through the sudden rising of a river which he had to pass in order to pay at the time fixed in his bond, the law asked simply whether he undertook to pay at that date and whether he paid accordingly. He took the risk of mischance, and the strict law did not undertake to act as his guardian. Again, the strict law had little use for one who was tricked or coerced into a legal transaction. It might allow him to sue for the wrong done. But it declined to set aside the transaction. If he could not guard his own interests, he must not ask the courts, which were only keeping the peace, to do so for him. When it did regard force and fraud, the law in this stage refused to regard the actual case and ask, was this man deceived or compelled? Instead it asked, would the standard, normal man have been defrauded or coerced by what was done? In other words, it held that every man of mature age must take care of himself. He need not expect to be saved from himself by legal paternalism or by legal maternalism. If he made a foolish bargain, it conceived he must perform his side like a man, for he had but himself to blame. When he acted, he was held to have acted at his own risk with his eyes open, and he must abide the appointed consequences. He must be a good sport and bear his losses smiling. The stock argument of the strict law for the many harsh rules it enforces is that the situation was produced by the party's own folly and he must abide it. The whole point of view is that of primitive society and recalls the story in Tacitus of how the Germans played dice. They played, he tells us, as a serious business, even staking their own liberty; and if one lost in such a case, he voluntarily went into slavery and patiently allowed himself to be sold. Something of this spirit, which is the spirit of the strict law, may be recognized today in such doctrines as contributory negligence and assumption of risk and the exaggerations of contentious procedure which treat litigation as a game.

Thus our Anglo-American law in its very beginning has in it the individualism of the strict law.

While the strict law insisted that every man should stand upon his own feet and should play the game as a man, without squealing, the principal social and legal institution of the time in which the common law was formative, the feudal relation of lord and man, regarded men in quite another way. Here the question was not what a man had undertaken or what he had done, but what he was. The lord had rights against the tenant and the tenant had rights against the lord. The tenant owed duties of service and homage or fealty to the lord, and the lord owed duties of defense and warranty to the tenant. And these rights existed and these duties were owing simply because the one was lord and the other was tenant. The rights and duties belonged to that relation. Whenever the existence of that relation put one in the class of lord or the class of tenant, the rights and duties existed as a legal consequence. The first solvent of individualism in our law and the chief factor in fashioning its system and many of its characteristic doctrines was the analogy of this feudal relation, suggesting the juristic conception of rights, duties and liabilities arising, not from express undertaking, the terms of any transaction, voluntary wrongdoing or culpable action, but simply and solely as incidents of a relation.

How important this conception is in the system of the common law may be perceived if we compare the

Roman and the Anglo-American way of putting things with respect to some of the everyday institutions of the law. In the Romanist system the chief rôle is played by the conception of a legal transaction, an act intended to create legal results to which the law carrying out the will of the actor gives the intended effect. The central idea in the developed Roman system is to secure and effectuate the will. All things are deduced from or referred to the will of the actor. Arising as the law of the city of Rome when it was a city of patriarchal households, and as a body of rules for keeping the peace among the heads of these households, its problem was to reconcile the conflicting activities of free men, supreme within their households but meeting and dealing with their equals without. Accordingly it held them in penalties for such injuries as they did wilfully and held them in obligations to such duties or performances as they undertook in legal form. It held them for what they willed and did willingly and it held them to what they willed and undertook legally. In our law, by contrast, the central idea is rather relation. Thus in agency, the civilian thinks of an act, a manifestation of the will, whereby one person confers a power of representation upon another, and of a legal giving effect to the will of him who confers it. Accordingly he talks of the contract of mandate. The common-law lawyer, on the other hand, thinks of the relation of principal and agent and of powers, rights, duties and liabilities, not as willed by the parties but as incident to and involved in the relation. He, therefore, speaks of the relation of principal and agent. So in partnership. The Romanist speaks of the contract of *societas*. He develops all his doctrines from the will of the parties who engaged in the legal transaction of forming the partnership, and he treats it when formed on the analogy of *communio* or common ownership in case of the *consortium* of coheirs who keep the patriarchal household undivided after the death of its head. We speak instead of the partnership relation and of the powers and rights and duties which the law attaches to that relation. Again, the Romanist speaks of a letting and hiring of land and of the consequences which are willed by entering into that contract. We speak of the law of landlord and tenant and of the warranties which it implies, the duties it involves and the incidents attached thereto. The Romanist speaks of a *locatio operarum,* a letting of services and of the effects which the parties have willed thereby. We speak of the relation of master and servant and of the duty to furnish safe appliances and the assumption of risk which are imposed upon the respective parties thereto. The Romanist speaks of family law. We speak of the law of domestic relations. The double titles of our digests, such as principal and surety, or vendor and purchaser, where the Romanist would use the one word, suretyship or sale, tell the same story.

Anglo-American law is pervaded on every hand by the idea of relation and of legal consequences flowing therefrom. At law, the original type which provided the analogy still exists in the law of landlord and tenant. If I occupy your land adversely, you may put me out and then have your action on the case for mesne profits; but you have no action against me for that I am enriched unjustly by the use and occupation of your land. The action for use and occupation may be maintained only where a relation exists. But when the relation does exist a train of legal consequences follow. There is an implied warranty of quiet enjoyment. There is an obligation to pay rent simply because of the relation, which the covenants in the lease only liquidate. Covenants in the lease run with the land; that is the incidents so created go with the relation, not with the person who made them. Again, in case of a conveyance for life there is still the relation of tenure, involving duties of the tenant toward those in reversion and remainder. Hence covenants are said to run with the land, that is, to follow the relation. But in case of a conveyance in fee simple there has been no relation since the statute of *Quia Emptores* in the reign of Edward I, and so the burden of covenants in the conveyance does not run. In the United States, when first we sought to extend the law as to the creation of legal servitudes by permitting such covenants to run, we did not break over the rule expressly, but our courts instead turned to the word "privity," which in its proper use refers to a relation, and thought the result justified by the conjuring up of a fictitious privity. So also in the law of torts, the existence of some special relation calling for care or involving a duty of care is often decisive of liability. For example, if A is drowning and B is sitting upon the bank with a rope and a life belt at hand, unless there is some relation between A and B other than that they are both human beings, for all that the law prescribes, B may smoke his cigarette and see A drown. In the absence of a relation that calls for action the duty to be the good Samaritan is moral only. Other systems may reach the result in another way. But here and in other places where it is much less legitimate, the common-law judge tends to seek for some relation between the parties, or as he is likely to put it, some duty of the one to the other.

Again in the case of mortgagor and mortgagee, we do not ask what the parties agreed, but we apply rules, such as once a mortgage always a mortgage, or such as the rule against clogging the equity of redemption, which defeat intent, in order to enforce the incidents which courts of equity hold involved in the relation. In the case of sale of land, it is not our mode of thought to consider that we are carrying out the will of the parties as manifested in their contract. Once the relation of vendor and purchaser is established, we think rather of the rights and duties involved in that relation, of the conversion of the contract right into an equitable ownership and the turning of the legal title of the vendor into a security for money, not because the parties so intended, but because the law, sometimes in the face of stipulations for a forfeiture, gives those effects to their relation. Then too, we have the great category of fiduciary relations, of which trustee and beneficiary is the type. It is true this category and many of the instances above recounted are the work not of common-law courts but of the courts of equity. But the common-law lawyer was at work in the courts of equity. The clerical chancellors brought about an infusion of morals into the legal system. To prevent dishonest or unconscientious conduct, interposing originally perhaps for the welfare of his soul, they forbade the trustee's or the fiduciary's doing this or that which legally he was at liberty to do. Presently common-law lawyers came to sit upon the woolsack. They turned at once to their staple analogy, lord and man, landlord and tenant, and out of the pious interference of the chancellors on general grounds of morals they built the category of fiduciary relations with rights and duties annexed to them and involved in them, no matter what the parties to the relation may intend. So completely has this idea taken possession of equity that more than one subject, for example interpleader and bills of peace, is embarrassed by a struggle to find "privity," a struggle to find some relation to which the right to relief may be annexed.

Our public law, too, is built around this same idea of relation. Magna Carta is recognized as the foundation of Anglo-American public law. But Professor Adams has shown that, as a legal document, Magna Carta is a formulation of the duties involved in the jural relation of the king to his tenants in chief. As the Middle Ages confused sovereignty and property, it was easy enough to draw an instrument declaring the duties incident to the relation of lord and man which, when the former happened to be king, could be made later to serve as defining the duties owing by the king in the relation of king and subject. Political theory sought to explain the duties of rulers and governments by a Romanist juristic theory of contract, a theory of a contract between sovereign and subjects which was devised originally in the medieval contests between church and state to justify disobedience on the part of the pious subject who resisted a royal contemner of ecclesiastical privileges. We shall see in another connection how in the eighteenth century the two theories merged and the common-law rights of Englishmen, involved in the relation of king and subject, became the natural rights of man deduced from a social compact. Here it suffices to note that the latter is an alien conception in our law. After working no little mischief in our constitutional law in the nineteenth century, this conception of natural rights going back of all constitutions and merely declared thereby is giving way and there are signs that we shall return to the true common-law conception of the rights and duties which the law imposes on or annexes to the relation of ruler and ruled.

Because of its origin in the general application to new problems of the analogy of the reciprocal rights and duties of lord and man, I have ventured to call this element of our legal tradition "feudal law." Perhaps it might be called "Germanic law." For in comparing Roman law and Germanic law, we are struck at once by differences of treatment of the same institution in the two systems, and these differences turn largely upon their respective use of will and of relation as fundamental notions. Compare for instance the Roman *patria potestas,* the power of the head of the household, with the corresponding Germanic institution of the *mundium.* The Roman institution is legally quite one-sided. The *paterfamilias* is legally supreme within the household. He has rights. But whatever duties he may owe are owed without the household, not within. On the other hand, the Germanic institution is conceived of as a relation of protection and subjection. But the subjection is not because of a right of the housefather. It is a subjection because of the relation and for the purposes of the protection which the relation involves. Also the right of the housefather grows out of the relation and is a right against the world to exercise his duty of protection. Indeed, Tacitus indicates to us this idea of relation as a characteristic Germanic institution. As such, it became the fundamental legal idea in the feudal social organization. In our law, however, the idea is a generalization from the results of judicial working out of one problem after another by the analogy of the institution with which courts were most familiar and had most to do in the formative period of English law, namely, the relation of lord and tenant.

In the nineteenth century the feudal contribution to the common law was in disfavor. Puritanism, the attitude of protecting the individual against government and society which the common-law courts had taken in the contests with the crown, the eighteenth-century theory of the natural rights of the abstract individual man, the insistence of the pioneer upon a minimum of interference with his freedom of action, and the nineteenth-century deduction of law from a metaphysical principle of individual liberty—all these combined to make jurists and lawyers think of individuals rather than of groups or relations and to make jurists think ill of anything that had the look of the archaic institution of *status*. The Romanist idea of contract became the popular juristic idea and, as Maitland puts it, contract became "the greediest of legal categories." Attempt was made to Romanize more than one department of Anglo-American law by taking for the central idea the Romanist doctrine of a legal giving effect to the individual will. This was furthered by the general acceptance in England and the United States of the political interpretation of jurisprudence and of legal history, an interpretation which found the key to social and hence to legal progress in a gradual unfolding of the idea of individual liberty in the progress of political institutions. It was furthered also by the famous generalization of Sir Henry Maine that the evolution of law is a progress from *status* to contract. Accepting this doctrine, English writers have charged that the common law is archaic because it refers legal consequences to relations rather than to contracts or to intention. But in truth the dogma of Sir Henry Maine is a generalization from Roman legal history only. It shows the course of evolution of Roman law. On the other hand it has no basis in Anglo-American legal history, and the whole course of English and American law today is belying it, unless indeed, we are progressing backward.

Taking no account of legislative limitations upon freedom of contract, in the purely judicial development of our law we have taken the law of insurance practically out of the category of contract, and we have established that the duties of public service companies are not contractual, as the nineteenth-century sought to make them, but are instead relational; they do not flow from agreements which the public servant may make as he chooses, they flow from the calling in which he has engaged and his consequent relation to the public. What is this in each case (and these are relatively recent developments of the law) but the common-law idea of relation, a relation of insurer and insured and of public utility and patron, and of rights, duties and liabilities involved therein? It is significant that progress in our law of public service companies has taken the form of abandonment of nineteenth-century views for doctrines which may be found in the Year Books.

Even more significant is the legislative development whereby duties and liabilities are imposed on the employer in the relation of employer and employee, not because he has so willed, not because he is at fault, but because the nature of the relation is deemed to call for it. Such is the settled tendency of the present. To me it seems a return to the common-law conception of the relation of master and servant, with reciprocal rights and duties and with liabilities imposed in view of the exigencies of the relation. Workmen's compensation acts have put jurists to much trouble when they have sought to find a place for them in the legal system. Some have said they create a *status* of being a laborer and this has frightened more than one court. For *status* is an archaic idea, quite out of line with modern ideas. Hence they have felt bound to inquire what warrant might be found for imposing disabilities upon one whom nature had given a sound mind, disposing judgment and years of discretion. Others have said that the duties and liabilities involved in workmen's compensation acts were quasi-contractual —which means only that the author did not know what to call them or where to place them. What is clear is that they are not contractual and that they are not in accord with what the last century regarded as the principles of the law of torts. Is this legislation, then, in opposition to our law of torts, so that one or the other must give way? If so, if this legislation may not be made to fit into the system of the common law, it may go hard with it in the judicial working out of its consequences. But I submit the common law has a place for it and that without disturbance of our legal system it is perfectly possible to administer these statutes and to give them the sympathetic judicial development which all statutes require, if they are to be effective. For it is not out of line with the common law to deal with causes where the relation of master and servant exists differently from causes where there is no such relation. It is not out of line to deal with such causes by determining the duties and the liabilities which shall flow from the relation. On the contrary, the nineteenth century was out of line with the common law when it sought to treat the relation of master and servant in any other way. In administering these acts the common law may employ its oldest and most fertile legal conception. Hence we may believe confidently that it will soon assimilate this legislation and develop it into an agency of justice.

It used to be said by way of reproach that the common law was feudal. The Roman idea of a legal transaction, which the nineteenth century sought to apply to all possible situations, was regarded as the legal institution of the maturity of law. But the conception of a legal transaction regards individuals only. In the pioneer agricultural societies of nineteenth-century America such a conception sufficed. In the industrial and urban society of today classes and groups and relations must be taken account of no less than individuals. Happily the nineteenth century did not lose for us the contribution of the feudal law to our legal tradition. In its idea of relation, in the characteristic common-law mode of treating legal problems which it derived from the analogy of the incidents of feudal tenure we have a legal institution of capital importance for the law of the future; we have a means of making our received legal tradition a living force for justice in the society of today and of tomorrow, as it was in the society of yesterday.

II

PURITANISM AND THE LAW

LEGAL history, as we now know it, began to be written after Savigny and so after Hegel. Hence the "great-man interpretation" of history which was superseded by Hegel's idealistic interpretation, has never played much part in the literature of law. The attributing of ancient "codes" to gods or to divinely inspired sages or the Greek and Roman practice of attributing a whole body of legal and political institutions to some one lawgiver are another matter. They represent an attempt to put symbolically the sacredness of the law or the antiquity and authority of the custom on which the general security rests, and their place is taken in modern times by an idea that our traditionally received body of law is based upon an eternal intrinsic reasonableness. Yet something might be said for a great-lawyer interpretation of legal history. One might attribute progress in legal institutions and the development of legal doctrines to the influence and the genius of leaders among juristic writers, judges and practising lawyers. Lord Campbell thought the lives of the Chancellors and of the Chief Justices might be made to tell the history of the English constitution and the history of English law. Not long ago a writer sought to give us the spirit of the classical Roman law through a study of the life and character of Papinian. Undoubtedly the great lawyer has not been the least factor in legal history. Roman law without Papinian and Ulpian and Paul, the civil law of the modern world without Bartolus, international law without Grotius, French law without Pothier, German law without Savigny, the common law without Coke, or American constitutional law without Marshall, are almost unthinkable. But it may be that lawyers are products of legal development or along with legal institutions and systems and doctrines are results of deeper-seated forces. It may be that the lawyers themselves call for interpretation. Historical jurists in the last century were wont to teach us that the contents of a legal system were a necessary result of the whole history of a people and were no more to be explained by the labors of individuals than was language. Later it was asserted that great jurists and great judges had been but the mouthpieces, through which social forces, or the civilization of the time and place or class struggle or economic pressure and the interest of the dominant class for the time being had spoken the law. Whichever of these views was accepted, the creative rôle of great lawyers was pushed into the background in legal history, and he would be a bold man today who would essay an exposition of the spirit of the common law by study of the judges through whose decisions our law has been expressed and has been given form.

But little has been done in the way of applying the other modes of interpreting legal history to the history of Anglo-American law. The idealistic interpretation, which looks upon the history of law as the unfolding of an idea of right or justice in human experience, has been employed with no little success in writing the history of Roman law. One phase of this, the religious interpretation, which seeks the key to juristic progress and juridical institutions in the progress of religious thought and in the progress of religious institutions, has been used in connection with Roman law by those who have attempted to trace the effect of Christianity upon the final stage of that system in the ancient world. Neither of these, however, has been tried by historians of the common law. Another phase of the idealistic interpretation, on the other hand, has been the staple of our books in the immediate past. Both in jurisprudence and in politics, the political interpretation has been the favorite in England and in America. Historically it assumes that a movement from subjection to freedom, from status to contract, is the key to legal as well as to social development. Philosophically it sees the end of all law in liberty and conceives of jurisprudence as the science of civil liberty. Given currency in the United States through the writings of Sir Henry Maine, this interpretation was no mean influence in bringing about the attitude of our courts and lawyers toward social legislation which often, but, as I think, erroneously, has been attributed to class interest. An ethnological interpretation, which finds the determining factors in juristic progress and in legal institutions in the characteristics of the races of men among whom laws exist, has been urged also. But the attempts to apply this method to the history of Roman law have yielded doubtful and meager results and there seems no reason to suppose that it will do more for the history of our law. Finally there is an economic interpretation which is much in vogue at present. Its exponents assert that the idea of justice has had nothing to do with the actual course of legal development, and contend that the sole agency in determining the growth and the content of legal systems has been the self interest of the class dominant for the time being in a particular society.

There is truth behind each of these several interpretations, and it would be hard to choose among them, if choice were necessary. But choice is not necessary. No social institution is the product of any one cause. It is rather the resultant of many causes, of which some observers will lay stress upon one and some upon others, but none of which may be left out of account. Hence if some tell us that the spirit of the common law, the exaggerated abstract individualism of our juristic thinking and judicial decision in the last century, is due to an innate tendency to individualism among Germanic peoples, kept down in some quarters by the weight of Roman authority, but never so repressed in England, while others see in it an outgrowth of the political contests between the courts and the crown in the sixteenth and seventeenth centuries and an outcome of the political development of that time; if some regard it as a product of Puritanism, an application of Puritan ideas in law and politics, reaching its highest development in America, that paradise of the Philistines, as Matthew Arnold put it, while others see instead a result of economic thought and economic conditions in nineteenth-century America and of the frontier spirit surviving the frontier, I do not think we are bound to make an absolute choice. In truth all of these are factors and more than one has been a factor of importance. Possibly one might refer Puritan theology and sixteenth- and seventeenth-century political thought ultimately to Germanic individualism. Kept back by Roman authority in law and in theology, the Germanic genius burst its bonds at the Reformation and the individual asserted himself in law, in politics, in philosophy and in religion. One might say that there was something congenial to the Germanic spirit in Hebraism which gave the Old Testament so profound an influence when our fathers began to read it. In that view the Germanic character plus the economic conditions of the past century and the resulting economic theories would be our formula. But one must reckon with the interaction of individualist character and religious doctrine and social conditions upon one another. There is little to be gained therefore by an attempt at broad generalization. We may say, at least, that Puritanism of itself and possibly because of the deeper-seated causes of which it was a manifestation, has been a significant factor in molding the spirit of our common law.

Indeed there are special reasons for believing that Puritanism has been in a sense a controlling factor. And these reasons are my excuse, at a time when religious interpretations are not the fashion, for venturing a bit of religious interpretation of jurisprudence. For individualism, in and of itself, has not been peculiarly English or peculiarly American. What is peculiar to Anglo-American legal thinking, and above all to American legal thinking, is an ultra-individualism, an uncompromising insistence upon individual interests and individual property as the focal point of jurisprudence. Other causes brought about a period of individualism in jurisprudence in politics and in economics everywhere. It was perhaps Puritanism which gave that added emphasis to individualist ideas in the formative period of our American legal thought that served to stamp them upon our theory and our practice and kept them alive and active in the United States a half century after English legal thought had turned over a new leaf. Upon this hypothesis, the religious interpretation of our legal thought becomes no less important than the philosophical interpretation of Roman law, through recognition of the part played by the Stoic philosophy in its formative period.

Individualism in legal science, as distinguished from law, had its origin in the end of the sixteenth century and beginning of the seventeenth century in the rise of theories of natural rights out of the older theories of natural law. Two main factors in this rise of individualism may be recognized, namely, the emancipation of the middle class and Protestantism. Berolzheimer has identified the former with the maturity and decay of the theory of natural law. But individualist natural law still flourishes in America. And if it be said that America has been *par excel-*

lence the country of the middle class, we must note that the middle class has been dominant elsewhere and that Puritanism has given a peculiar character to the middle class of England and America. Even less may we attribute our common-law mode of thought solely to the Protestantism of England in the period which was decisive for modern law. For one thing its attitude toward the State is quite as much Catholic as Protestant. It is much nearer the view of the Jesuit jurists of the Counter-Reformation than it is to the view of Luther and his followers. In politics, Luther's principle was passive obedience. Holding that submission to civil government was enjoined upon Christians by the Scriptures, both Luther and Melanchthon vigorously denounced the Anabaptists and the rebellious peasants. Indeed they assumed that the state was a chief good and that no individual claims could stand against it. The basis for this doctrine was nationalist rather than individualist. They insisted on the local sovereign as against the universal church and the Protestant jurist theologians who followed them insisted upon the national law proceeding from that sovereign as against the universal authority of Rome. Granting that it was the mission of the Reformation to "give life to individual freedom," individual freedom through the state and through society were quite as possible means of achieving this mission as the Anglo-American exaltation of abstract individual freedom above the state and above society. In other words, a peculiar phase of the emancipation of the middle class and a peculiar phase of Protestantism must be taken account of in order to understand the spirit of our common law.

It is not an accident that the first reformer in English legal thought was also the first reformer in English religious thought. John Wycliffe is known for his resistance to authority in the church and his translation of the Scriptures to bring them home to the common man. But in his tract *De Officio Regis* he attacked authority in law and asserted the sufficiency of English case law—for such it fairly had become—against the venerable legislation of Justinian and the sacred decretals of the Popes. Let us remember what this meant according to the theories of that time. Whatever the fact, the theory of the king's judges was that they administered the common custom of England, the customary modes of action of Englishmen in their relations with each other. The academic theory as to the Roman law was that the *Corpus Iuris Ciuilis,* as legislation of the Emperor Justinian, was binding upon peoples whose rulers were taken to be successors of Augustus. The theory as to the canon law was that all jurisdiction was divided between the spiritual and the temporal, that in matters spiritual the temporal authority was wholly incompetent, and that the church, whose mouthpiece was the Pope, had an absolute legislative power within this field. "The Pope," says Boniface VIII in the fourteenth century, "holds all laws in his breast." Wycliffe said boldly that men might well be saved "though many laws of the Pope had never been spoken," that Roman law was "heathen men's law" and that there was no more reason and justice in the civil law of Rome than in the civil law of England. He appealed from authority to the local custom of England, from the rules imposed externally by Roman law and the Pope, to the rules which Englishmen made for themselves by their everyday conduct. But this was the same position which Wycliffe took with respect to religion. In law and in religion he appealed to the individual and for the individual against authority.

But the real influence of religious thinking was to come later. It has been said that for most purposes the history of the common law begins in the latter part of the thirteenth century. Indeed it might well be said that for American purposes its history begins still later and that we shall not err greatly in beginning with the end of the sixteenth century. I am speaking here of the common law as a mode of thought. Some dogmas, especially in the law of property, have a longer history, and our judicial institutions must be studied from the time of Henry II. But our attitude toward legal problems, our modes of legal reasoning, the principles which make up the system of the common law, have only to be studied from the reign of Elizabeth, and have a continuous and consistent development from that time. The periods of development in Anglo-American law begin respectively with the reigns of Elizabeth and James I, with the American Revolution and with the Civil War.

What had been achieved in the English courts prior to Coke was summed up for us and handed down to us by that indefatigable lawyer in a form which the past generation chose to consider authoritative; and we have looked at it through his spectacles ever since. Hence the period of growth prior to the reigns of Elizabeth and James I but gave the materials. The shape which those materials have taken in the present law is due to the way in which their possibilities appealed to the end of the sixteenth century and beginning of the seventeenth century, to the interpretation put on them by Coke and his contemporaries, and to the subsequent working over of the product in America when we received such part of the common law as was applicable to the new world. Again, we may pass over the constructive work of the eighteenth century, for that work was done in equity and the law merchant. Neither of these strictly is part of the common law, and so far from their affecting the spirit of the common law, the spirit of the common law affects them powerfully. But there are two growing periods of our common-law system; two periods in which rules and doctrines were formative, in which our authorities summed up the past for us and gave us principles for the future. These periods are (1) the classical common-law period, the end of the sixteenth and beginning of the seventeenth century, and (2) the period that some day, when the history of the common law as a law of the world comes to be written, will be regarded as no less classical than the first—the period of legal development in the United States that came to an end with the Civil War. In the one the task was to go over the decisions and legislation of the past and make a system for the future. In the other the task was to examine the whole body of English case law with reference to what was applicable to the facts of life in America and what was not. Obviously the spirit of these times and of the men of these times whose juristic labors gave us the mode of treating legal problems which we call the common law, could not fail to give color to the whole system. But the age of Coke was the age of the Puritan in England and the period that ends with our Civil War was the age of the Puritan in America. We must not forget that the Puritan had his own way in America, that he was in the majority, that he had no powerful establishment to contend with, and that he made institutions to his own liking. For, again, it is not an accident that common-law principles, as they were fashioned in the age of Coke, have attained their highest and most complete logical development in America, and that in this respect we are and long have been more thoroughly a common-law country than England herself.

A fundamental proposition from which the Puritan proceeded was the doctrine of a "willing covenant of conscious faith" made by the individual. Thus he put individual conscience and individual judgment in the first place. No authority might rightfully coerce them; but everyone must assume and abide the consequences of the choice he made. Applied to church polity, it led to a régime of "consociation but not subordination." "We are not over one another," said Robinson, "but with one another." Hence even church organization was a species of contract and a legal theory, a legalism, attached even to religion. If men were to be free to act according to their consciences and to contract with others for consociation in congregations, it was a necessary consequence that the state, as a political congregation, was a matter of contract also; and liberty of contract was a further necessary deduction. The early history of New England furnishes abundant applications of the idea that covenant or compact—the consent of every individual to the formation and to the continuance of the community—was the basis of all communities, political as well as religious. The precedent of the covenant which made Abraham and the children of Israel the people of God, furnished the religious basis for the doctrine. But it was applied to civil as well as to ecclesiastical organization. One consequence was to make for the individualistic conception that all legal consequences depend upon some exertion of the will, as against the feudal conception of referring them to some relation. Contract and voluntary culpable conduct appeared to be the solving ideas for all problems and the law was to be apportioned between the contractual and the delictual. Another consequence was to make a moral question of everything, and yet in such a way as to make it a legal question. For moral principles are of individual and relative application. In applying them we must take account of circumstances and of individuals. Hence if every question was treated as a moral question and controversies involving moral questions were to be dealt with as concrete cases to be individualized in their solution, subordination of those whose cases were decided to those who had the power of weighing the circumstances of the actual case and individualizing the principle to meet the case might result. The idea of consociation demanded that a fixed, absolute, universal rule, which the individual had contracted to abide, be resorted to; and thus the moral and the legal principle were to be applied in the same way, and that the legal way. "Nowhere," says Morley, "has Puritanism done us more harm than in this leading us to take all breadth and color and diversity and fine discrimination out of our judgments of men, reducing them to thin, narrow and superficial pronouncements upon the letter of their morality or the precise conformity of their opinions to accepted standards of truth." The good side of all this we know well. On the side of politics, the conception of the people not as a mass but as an aggregate of individuals, the precise ascription of rights to each of these individuals, the evolution of the legal rights of Englishmen into the natural rights of man, have their immediate origin in the religious phase of the Puritan Revolution. But on the side of law, it has given us the conception of abstract liberty of contract, which has been the bane of all social legislation, the rooted objection to all power of equitable application of rules to concrete cases that has produced a decadence of equity in our state courts, the insistence upon and faith in the mere machinery of justice, which so often makes American legal procedure intolerable in the business world of today, the notion of punishing the vicious will and the necessary connection between wrongdoing and retribution, which makes it so difficult for our criminal law to deal with anti-social actions and to adjust itself in its application to the exigencies of concrete criminality.

How does this Puritan individualism affect the actual administration of justice? We may best answer by turning to each of the great departments of law and seeing the Puritan there at work. "The mission of the Reformation," says Berolzheimer, "was to give life to individual freedom." In this the Puritan is the incarnation of the Reformation. Individual freedom of interpretation, individual free association, individual rights were the basis of his religious, political and legal views. But abstract individual free self-assertion and individual interests are by no means all that legal systems have to look to, and in the nineteenth century our law showed on every side the ill effects of taking these for the sole basis. For instance, few doctrines of the common law create more impatience with courts today than the traditional attitude toward legislation, the judicial assumption that legislatures are in what Dicey calls the quiescent stage, the professional feeling that there ought to be little or no legislation on legal subjects, the attitude of resentment toward legislation on the part of bench and bar that has led so often to the failure of legislative attempts to simplify procedure, and has made so much of the labor of social workers nugatory after they have put it upon our statute books. For many years a favorite topic of presidential addresses before the American Bar Association was the plethora of legislature-made laws. A late leader of the American bar died in the harness writing an elaborate argument against legislation, and made generous provision in his will for a professorship in a law school whose incumbent should teach—I had almost said preach—the gospel of the futility of legislation. There is more than one reason for the attitude of the common law toward legislation. But not the least is the dominance of the Puritan during the formative periods of our law. His reasons were primarily religious. It appeared to him, says Lord Acton, "that governments and institutions are made to pass away like things of earth, whilst souls are immortal; that there is no more proportion between liberty and power than between eternity and time; that, therefore, the sphere of enforced command ought to be restricted within fixed limits and that which had been done by authority and outward discipline and organized violence, should be attempted by division of power and committed to the intellect and the conscience of free men."

Such views of law-making fitted into and confirmed common-law ideas which grew up in an age of legislative quiescence and were fostered by the masterful temperament of Edward Coke, who, brooking no lay interference with the law he had dug laboriously from the parchments of the past, impressed his ideas upon the tradition of which he was the authoritative exponent. Hence the orthodox tradition of our law schools wholly ignores the enacted element in law. In its teaching the older element, represented by the traditional course of decision, stands for the real law and furnishes principles and analogies, while the newer element, represented by legislation, is regarded as something alien, intruding in the body of the law, and may furnish only detailed rules for the cases expressly covered. Yet, while confirming the lawyer in his attitude toward legislation, the Puritan was a firm believer in enactment. The Commonwealth in England brought forth a great outburst of legislative activity. One of the first fruits of Massachusetts was an attempt to set the statute book in order. This colonial code of statute law antedates the revision of English legislation some two hundred years; and its preface contains a defense of legislative lawmaking. For, if the Puritan did not believe in coercion he did believe in instruction; and liberal instruction through the statute book, with the extent to which the instruction shall be followed left largely to the conscience and judgment of the individual, has long been an unhappy feature of our polity.

In the law of torts, few doctrines have been more irritating than those of assumption of risk and contributory negligence, as applied to injuries to employees. But these are eminently Puritan conceptions. The employee is a free man, guided by his own conscience and his own interpretation of Scripture. He chooses for himself. So choosing, he elects to work in a dangerous employment in which he runs a risk of being injured. He knows that others are to be employed with him; he knows that they may be negligent and that if they are, he may be injured. Very well; he is a free man, let him bear the loss. The master has done no wrong. The servant, to use Mr. Carter's language, must stand or fall by the consequences of his own conduct. It is not an accident that the classical exposition of this doctrine was penned in Massachusetts. Again, a workman, engaged constantly upon a machine, so that he comes to be a part of it and to operate mechanically himself, omits a precaution and is injured. The common law says to him, "You are a free man, you have a mind and are capable of using it; you chose freely to do a dangerous thing and were injured; you must abide the consequences." As a matter of fact, it may well be he did not and could not choose freely. Before the days of workmen's compensation it was said that statistics showed the great majority of industrial accidents happened in the last working hour of the day, when the faculties were numbed and the operative had ceased to be the free agent which our theory contemplated. But there was no escape from the legal theory. That very condition was a risk of the employment, and was assumed by the laborer. Legislation has been changing these rules, yet courts long had a tendency to read the doctrine of contributory negligence into statutes even where the legislature had tried to get rid of it.

Out of many examples in constitutional law, we may notice the nineteenth-century decisions as to the right to pursue a lawful calling and liberty of contract, which bore so grievously upon social legislation until well into the present century. Here it is significant that the prophet of a belated individualist crusade, the late Mr. Justice Field, had added to a Puritan ancestry and Puritan bringing up, careful study of the common law and practice of his profession on the frontier at a time and in a place where the individual counted for more and the law for less than has been usual even on the frontier. No doubt the latter circumstance had its influence. None the less the conception of a maximum of abstract individual self-assertion exempt from social control, to which his vigorous and learned opinions gave currency, is essentially the Puritan conception of consociation. We are to be with one another but not over one another. The whole is to have no right of control over the individual beyond the minimum necessary to keep the peace. Everything else is to be left to the free contract of a free man. Happily this idea passed its meridian in our constitutional law at the end of the last century.

Again in criminal law, one of the problems is the individualization of punishment, the adjusting of our penal system to the criminal rather than to the abstract crime. Another is to get rid of the retributive theory, the revenge idea as the basis of legal treatment of crime—an idea which is the bane of punitive justice. Still another is to make the criminal law an effective agency for repressing antisocial actions and protecting society. At each of these points our Puritan common-law theories have been fighting a vigorous defense and slow retreat.

The Puritan's objection to individualization in punitive justice was instinctive and deep-seated, for he saw in the Star Chamber the same fundamental theory as that involved in the penitential system of the Roman church. Sociologists are now recognizing the deep and humane insight of the ecclesiastical law and its essentially modern point of view. In the penitential system, "it is not the crime," says Saleilles, "but the criminal alone that is . . . regarded. It becomes a subjective individualization under cover of a wholly objective legal sentence; and this is what we now demand." "This subjective individualization," he continues, "is the same formula which is called for today." To the Puritan, such a point of view was wholly repugnant. The same attitude toward law and government that called for an over-individualism in the abstract rules of law and in the doctrines from which they proceed, precluded individualization or adjustment to individual cases in the application of the rules and doctrines in practice. In the former it is an assertion of the individual against his fellows individually. It expresses the feeling of the self-reliant man that he is to make his own bargains and determine upon his own acts and control his own property, accepting the responsibility that goes with such power, subjecting himself to liability for the consequences of his free choice, but exempt from interference in making his choice. In the latter it is an assertion of the individual against his fellows collectively. It expresses the feeling of the same self-reliant man that neither the state nor its representative, the magistrate, is competent to judge him better than his own conscience; that he is not to be judged by the discretion of men, but by the inflexible rule of the strict law.

Our criminal law had a new birth in the seventeenth century, when the fall of the Star Chamber threw the whole subject of punitive justice into the common-law courts. Accordingly it received the Puritan stamp while it was formative, and in the nineteenth century many of the United States carried the Puritan repugnance to all margin of judicial action so far as to abolish common-law misdemeanors and try to prescribe chapter and verse of a criminal code for every case. All three of the demands of modern criminal science, then, have been resisted by our Puritan criminal law. It is not so long ago that a learned supreme court released a child from a reformatory on the ground that a reformatory was a prison, that commitment thereto was necessarily punishment for crime, and hence could only be warranted by criminal proceedings of a formal type, conducted with due regard to constitutional safeguards. The rise of juvenile courts has accustomed us to courts of criminal equity for the youthful offender; but attempts to introduce any system of judicial individualization for the adult will have to wrestle a long time with constitutional difficulties. Indeed we have had to resort to administrative boards and commissions to do what England now does through a court of criminal appeal. So, too, the retributive theory is among the fundamenta of our criminal law. The common law looks upon the criminal in the abstract. He is a free man, who, having a choice between right and wrong, voluntarily chose the wrong and must abide the penal consequences appointed in advance. Not only does this Puritan view of the matter keep alive the retributive theory in jurisprudence, after kindred sciences have abandoned it, but it hampers the efficiency of penal legislation intended to protect society. The good sense of courts has introduced a doctrine of acting at one's peril with respect to statutory crimes which expresses the needs of society. Such statutes are not meant to punish the vicious will but to put pressure upon the thoughtless and inefficient to do their whole duty in the interest of public health or safety or morals. Nevertheless all extension of this doctrine has been opposed sturdily by our text-writers, and to the Puritanism of Bishop and common-law orthodoxy of Judge McClain the decisions are anomalous and unsatisfactory.

In the law of property we may see conspicuous examples in the doctrine as to "abusive exercise of rights"—as to use of property or exercise of powers incident to property for the sole purpose of injuring another—and in the older doctrine with respect to surface water. Here again we may note that the typical exposition of the extreme individualist view as to the rights of adjoining owners in disposing of surface water came from Massachusetts. Much of this has been done away with under modern Roman influence. But the common law asked simply, was the defendant acting on his own land and committing no nuisance? If so, it cared nothing about his motive. If one were to put the argument of the French jurists, that use of property merely to injure another is anti-social and should be repressed, the common-law lawyer would no doubt reply in the language of Blackstone, "the public good is in nothing more essentially interested than in the protection of every individual's private rights."

Equity in America shows the same influence. The Puritan has always been a consistent and thoroughgoing opponent of equity. It runs counter to all his ideas. For one thing, it helps fools who have made bad bargains, whereas he believes that fools should be allowed and required to act freely and then be held for the consequences of their folly. For another thing, it acts directly upon the person. It coerces the individual free will. It acts preventively, instead of permitting free action and imposing after the event the penalty assented to in advance. For still another, it involves discretion in its application to actual cases, and that, in the Puritan view, means superiority in the magistrate in that it allows him to judge another by a personal standard instead of by an unyielding, impersonal, legal rule. Hence in large part the opposition to the Court of Chancery in England, which lasted almost to the eighteenth century, the abolition of the Court of Chancery by Barebones' Parliament and the tracts against chancery during the Commonwealth. Hence the reluctance of Massachusetts to grant equity powers to the courts and the popular vote against equity in New Hampshire after the Revolution. Hence the general tendency in the United States to turn the liberal doctrines of equity as to discretion in granting relief into hard and fast jurisdictional rules. Pomeroy has remarked "the extreme reluctance of American courts to extend the jurisdiction of equity, even where such extension consists solely in applying familiar principles to new conditions of fact." The gradual abandonment of equity powers and legalizing of equitable doctrines which I have ventured on another occasion to call a decadence of equity in America is no less remarkable. Truly the methods and doctrines of equity have not been congenial to our tribunals, and if we remember that the latter have been manned with Puritans, the reason is obvious.

From the beginning the Protestant tradition in law has been nationalist. The Protestant jurist theologians of the sixteenth and seventeenth centuries opposed a nationalist conception to the universal authority of the canon law and the universal doctrines of the Jesuit jurists of the Counter-Reformation. For universal authority, they sought to substitute the civil law of each people, sacred because it sprang from the divinely ordained state. The Puritan carried this particularism in law to the extreme because of his conception of states as political congregations. The Ten Commandments and the Scriptures, interpreted by the individual Christian, furnished sufficient general principles. For the rest, there was need only of the local laws to which those subject thereto had freely assented. Much of this spirit is with us today in the American exaltation of local peculiarities in law, in our fostering of local anomalies of substantive law and of procedure as if they had some intrinsic importance in the administration of justice to compensate for the manifold inconveniences to which they give rise. Until the general adoption of the Negotiable Instruments Law, it used to be a saying in the West that a draft on Chicago drawn in Omaha and put through the usual course of collection was subject to three different laws. Nor did this seem incongruous to lawyers. Even now that, under pressure from business men, the uniform Negotiable Instruments Law has been put in force, so little does the common-law lawyer value universality, that there are disquieting symptoms of provincial interpretations in the several states which will involve a gradual return to our former condition of divergent local laws.

It is, however, in application and administration of the law that Puritanism has produced the most serious results for the legal system of today. The Puritan's characteristic jealousy of the magistrate has taken an extreme form and has been developed as a jealousy of the judge. "There is," says Bryce, "a hearty Puritanism in the view of human nature which pervades [the Constitution]. It is the work of men who believed in original sin, and were resolved to leave open for transgressors no door which they could possibly shut." It is hardly too much to say that the Puritan ideal state was a permanent deadlock where the individual, instructed by a multitude of rules but not coerced, had free play for the dictates of his own reason and conscience. For our legislation exhibits an inconsistency that is part of the Puritan character. He rebelled against control of his will by state or magistrate, yet he loved to lay down rules, since he realized the intrinsic sinfulness of human nature. Accordingly we have abundance of rules and no adequate provision for carrying them out. Until we began to find a way out by our recent development of administrative boards and commissions, law paralyzed administration. In the nineteenth century injunctions, actions of trespass, and mandamus proceedings hemmed in the executive officer on every side. But when the judicial department came forward to execute laws, local juries and grand juries, local prosecuting officers, local sheriffs, were given power to hold up as well as to uphold the law and wielded it as their individual consciences might dictate. Hence it was no less true that administration paralyzed law. The system of checks and balances produced a perfect balance. In practical result, the law too often accomplished little or nothing. We had abundance of law in the books, but very little law in action. Revolt from this condition, which had become intolerable in our complex urban societies at the end of the last century has almost threatened a season of oriental justice through conferring of wide powers upon boards and commissions which are expected to proceed with a minimum of rule and a maximum of expedition.

Puritan jealousy of the magistrate is even more

conspicuous in American judicial procedure. It has coöperated with the pioneer spirit and the ideas of rural communities in the first half of the nineteenth century to produce a condition in the administration of judicial business very like that to which it led in executive administration. In more than one state codes and practice acts aim to regulate every act of the judge from the time he enters the court room. It is hardly too much to say that the ideal judge is conceived as a pure machine. Being a human machine and in consequence tainted with original sin, he must be allowed no scope for free action. Hard and fast rules of evidence and strict review of every detail of practice by a series of reviewing tribunals are necessary to keep him in check. In many states he may not charge the jury in any effective manner; he must rule upon and submit or reject written requests for academically-phrased propositions of abstract law; he must not commit any error which might possibly prejudice a party to the cause—whether in fact there is prejudice or not. The past two decades have seen a steady movement away from this type of procedure; but in more than one Western community, settled from New England, which preserves the pristine faith, it is dying hard. Dunning has pointed out that in America the Puritan was able to carry into effect what in England could be only abstract opinions. Hence in America, in addition to a ritual of justice belonging to a past age of formalism that put gold lace and red coats on the picket line, we have a machinery of justice devised to keep down the judicial personality which has made legal procedure in some sort an end in itself.

At the beginning of the present century it had become evident that our legal system must temper its individualism; that the common law could not succeed in an attempt to force the modern world into a Puritan bed of Procrustes. We may grant that the law should only temper, not abandon, the element in our tradition which was contributed by the Puritan. In another connection I shall try to show how we may use that element in the legal development of the future. But for the moment we must insist upon keeping it within bounds. If we recognize that it is not fundamental principles of jurisprudence, but traditional principles of Puritanism, operating out of their sphere, with which American legislatures are struggling, we may abate some of our hostility to legislation, and may be willing to allow lawmakers to take account of the demands involved in social life and formulate in laws the needs of crowded urban industrial communities even in derogation of our traditional law. We may be willing to concede something to the *vir bonus* upon the woolsack who would protect men from themselves. We may be willing to allow the magistrate some power of meeting the exigencies of justice in concrete cases. We may be willing to trust a trial judge to use honestly and impartially the discretion without which trials will always be dilatory, expensive, and unsatisfactory. For it is always to be remembered that justice is made up of individual cases. If the judicial machinery does not produce speedy, inexpensive and just results in the actual causes that pass through it, no amount of mechanical or theoretical perfection will atone. Above all, we may be willing to relegate procedure to its proper place in the legal system.

At the battle of Balaclava the English pickets posted to warn their comrades of the approach of the enemy were themselves surprised, and the attack of the Russians on the main body was in progress before the pickets were aware that an enemy was in the neighborhood. In commenting on this, a military historian says that the surprise resulted from the high degree of drill and discipline of the pickets, which had destroyed all initiative and had led them to believe that they had done their whole duty when they had conformed to the rules in which they had been trained while on guard in barracks and parade grounds. The historian adds that rules may deaden men's wits but can hardly sharpen them.

Legal formulas are necessary to preserve the dignity of the tribunal, to expedite its business, to keep the person of the magistrate in due bounds, and to give to the judge the benefit of the experience of the past. But they are means, not ends. However much it may have suited the Puritan disposition to make them ends, in order to bring about a maximum of individual self-assertion and a minimum of magisterial action, it is against the genius of the time and the interest of the modern industrial community to continue in this attitude.

III

THE COURTS AND THE CROWN

ON a memorable Sunday morning, the 10th of November, 1612, the judges of England were summoned before King James I upon complaint of the Archbishop of Canterbury. It appeared that the High Commission, an administrative tribunal established for the regulation of the church, had begun to take cognizance of temporal matters and to deal with lay offenders. Not only was this tribunal wholly unknown to the common law, but it decided according to no fixed rules and subject to no appeal. When, accordingly, it sought to send its pursuivant to the house of this or that lay subject and arrest him upon a complaint of a wholly temporal nature, the Court of Common Pleas stopped the proceeding with a writ of prohibition. To meet this judicial insistence upon the supremacy of law, it was suggested that the king might take away from the judges any cause he pleased and decide it himself; and the immediate business of the Sunday morning conference with the judges was to explain this proposition and hear what they could say to it. The Archbishop proceeded to expound the alleged royal prerogative, saying that the judges were but the delegates of the king, wherefore the king might do himself, when it seemed best to him, what he left usually to these delegates. He added that this was clear, if not in law yet beyond question in divinity, for it could be shown from the word of God in the Scripture. To this Coke answered on behalf of the judges, that by the law of England the king in person could not adjudge any cause; all cases, civil and criminal, were to be determined in some court of justice according to the law and custom of the realm. "But," said the king, "I thought law was founded upon reason, and I and others have reason as well as the judges." "True it was," Coke responded, "that God had endowed his Majesty with excellent science and great endowments of nature; but his Majesty was not learned in the laws of his realm of England, and causes which concern the life or inheritance or goods or fortunes of his subjects are not to be decided by natural reason, but by the artificial reason and judgment of the law, which law is an art which requires long study and experience before that a man can attain to the cognizance of it." At this the king was much offended, saying that in such case he should be under the law, which it was treason to affirm. Coke answered in the words attributed to Bracton, that the king ought not to be under any man but under God and the law. But this was not the last of such conferences and in the end Coke, who would give no pledge to do otherwise than administer the law as a judge should, was removed.

In 1787 the legislature of Rhode Island, having put forth paper money of the nominal value of £100,000 made it penal to refuse to accept the bills in payment of articles offered for sale or to make any distinction between them and gold or silver coin and provided further that if any one were accused of that heinous offence, he should be tried forthwith in an inferior court by judges without a jury, on a summary complaint, without any continuance and with no appeal. One Weeden being charged with violating the statute objected that trial before such a special court uncontrolled by the supreme judiciary and without a jury was repugnant to the charter which stood as the constitution of the state, and hence that the statute was void. The judges sustained this objection. Thereupon, on the last Monday of September, 1787, the judges were summoned to appear before the legislature much as Coke and his colleagues had appeared before James I. The judges appeared and two of them made learned and convincing arguments that they could not be compelled by statute to send a citizen to jail without trial by jury when trial by jury was guaranteed by the constitution, the supreme law of the state, under which the legislature itself was constituted. The legislature, however, voted that it was not satisfied with the reasons of the judges, and a motion to dismiss the judges from their offices followed and would doubtless have prevailed had it not appeared that the constitution unhappily required the deliberate process of impeachment. Like cases occurred at the time in many states.

Again in the twentieth century, in the movement for recall, judges were to be sent for to explain themselves to the sovereign. Bills of rights in our constitutions, state and federal, had been administered by courts as the supreme law which they purport to be. Thereupon the people were urged to send for the judges, to determine that their reasons were unsatisfactory and to dismiss them. The alternative proposition was that the people proceed to decide the case directly, as James I sought to do.

There is a close parallel here in more senses than one. In the seventeenth century, it was progressive to insist upon the royal prerogative. Those who thought of the king as the guardian of social interests and wished to give him arbitrary power, that he might use it benevolently in the general interest, were enraged to see the sovereign tied down by antiquated legal bonds discovered by lawyers in such musty and dusty parchments as Magna Carta. To them, the will of the king was the criterion of law and it was the duty of the courts, whenever the royal will for the time being and for the cause in hand was ascertained, to be governed accordingly, since the judges were but the king's delegates to administer justice. In the eighteenth century, the center of political gravity had shifted to the legislature. That body now thought of itself as sovereign and conceived that, no matter what the terms of the fundamental law under which it sat, the courts had but to ascertain and give effect to its will. At the end of the nineteenth century the center of political gravity had shifted to the majority or more often the plurality of the electorate, voting at a given election, and those who thought of pluralities and militant minorities as the guardians of social interests and would give them arbitrary powers, that they might use them benevolently in the general interest, were enraged to see the sovereign tied down by what seemed to them dead precedents and antiquated legal bonds discovered by lawyers in eighteenth-century bills of rights. The judges were but delegates of the people to do justice. Therefore, it was conceived, they were delegates of the majority or plurality that stood for the whole in wielding general governmental powers. Once more it was insisted that the will of the ruling organ of the state, even for the time being and the cause in hand, must be both the ultimate guide and the immediate source to which judges should refer.

Toward king, legislature and plurality of the electorate, the common law has taken the same attitude. Within the limits in which the law recognizes them as supreme it has but to obey them. But it reminds them that they rule under God and the law. And when the fundamental law sets limits to their authority or bids them proceed in a defined path, the common-law courts have consistently refused to give effect to their acts beyond those limits. Juristically this attitude of the common-law courts, which we call the doctrine of the supremacy of law, has its basis in the feudal idea of the relation of king and subject and the reciprocal rights and duties involved therein. Historically, it goes back to a fundamental notion of Germanic law. Philosophically, it is a doctrine that the sovereign and all the agencies thereof are bound to act upon principles, not according to arbitrary will; are obliged to conform to reason, instead of being free to follow caprice.

Along with the doctrine of judicial precedent and trial by jury this doctrine of the supremacy of law is one of the three distinctively characteristic institutions of the Anglo-American legal system. It became definitely established therein as a result of the contests between the courts and the crown in the sixteenth and seventeenth centuries. Hence we may enquire (1) what led up to these contests, (2) what effect did they have on the common-law tradition, and, in particular, how did they contribute to the exaggerated individualism of that tradition in the nineteenth century, and (3) what is the significance of the resulting doctrine of the supremacy of law for the law of the future?

Throughout the Germanic law books of the Middle Ages, says Heusler, runs the idea that law is "a quest of the creature for the justice and truth of his creator." All notion of arbitrary will was foreign to it. The conception that the will of the sovereign had the force of law came from Rome, if not, indeed, from Byzantium. The Germanic conception was instead that expressed in the phrase attributed to Bracton—that the king was under God and the law. The Germanic polity always postulated a fundamental law above and beyond mere will. Moreover it conceived that those who wielded authority should be held to account for the conformity of their acts to that law. Perhaps the extreme instance is to be found in the Salic law, which prescribes that where a creditor has duly appealed to the count for justice and the count does not act with no sufficient reason, he shall answer with his life or redeem himself with his *wergeld;* but when he does act pursuant to such an appeal, if he goes beyond enforcement of what was due he is likewise to answer with his life or redeem himself with his *wergeld.* But the conception developed as the basis of public law only in England. There the establishment of strong central courts, purporting to administer the common custom of the whole realm, the strong central administrative power of the king, and the early formulations of the feudal duties of the king toward his tenants in chief afforded a unique opportunity for the evolution of a legal doctrine of the legal duties and responsibilities of those who wield governmental powers.

Two cases of the reign of Edward III show the first phase of the doctrine. In 1338 in an action of replevin for cattle distrained by a collector of the king's taxes, it appeared that the collector had no warrant under seal. The plaintiff demurred to his avowry (that is to his plea that he took as collector of taxes) and the court rendered judgment for the plaintiff. Men could not go about the realm distraining the property of the subject or purporting to collect the king's taxes without a special warrant. The next year, the Court of King's Bench, having convicted Reginald de Nerford and others of a forcible disseisin, issued a writ of *exegi facias* (outlawry) against them. This writ was returned by the sheriff who reported that he had received a letter from the king under his private seal to the effect that he had pardoned the defendants and commanding that they should not be put to damage, wherefore he had not executed the writ. The court would not listen to this. It told the sheriff he could not justify refusal to execute a writ of the king's court by showing a mere private letter from the king; and after imposing a fine upon the sheriff, it issued a new writ to outlaw the defendants. In other words, Edward III, King of England, might pardon offenders, but he might not instruct a sheriff to disobey the precepts of the law. If he did, the sheriff could not justify his disobedience thereby. When he acted as king, his acts were those of the law; when he acted by private letter as Edward Plantagenet, he could not interfere with the due course of the law which bound the whole realm. It will be noted that in each of these cases the point was largely one of form. If the tax collector had held a warrant in due form, if the king had pardoned Reginald de Nerford and his companions in the mode which the law recognized, there would have been no question. Yet there was more here than form. Requiring the king and his agents to act in due form, if their acts were to have legal validity, was, in an age of formal law, the first step toward requiring him and them to act within the legally appointed limits of their authority. When Fortescue wrote in praise of the laws of England a century later, he could lay down dogmatically that the power of the English king was not regal, in the sense that he could make what innovations and alterations in the laws he pleased and impose on his subjects what burdens he chose, but was instead political; it was not the personal government of Edward or Henry, it was the political government of the king of England, exercised within the bounds which the law and customs of the realm had established. In this wider form, the doctrine soon required the courts to pass on the validity of royal acts of a very different character.

At common law the king is *parens patriae,* father of his country, which is but the medieval mode of putting what we mean today when we say that the state is the guardian of social interests. In the feudal way of looking at it, the relation of king and subject involved duties of protection as well as rights to allegiance. The king, then, was charged with the duty of protecting public and social interests, and he wielded something very like our modern police power. But this power was limited on every side by the maxims of the common law and the bounds set by the law of the land. It was a maxim that the law had so admeasured the prerogatives of the king that they should neither take away nor prejudice the inheritance of anyone. Naturally the royal power of protecting social interests soon came in conflict with such a maxim. A few examples are worth recalling. Henry IV granted the measuring of woollen cloth or canvas that should be brought to London by any stranger or denizen, taking a penny of the buyer and another of the seller for each piece measured. The judges held that this was not a grant in the public interest; that it tended to the burdening, oppressing and impoverishing of the king's subjects and not to their advantage, "and therefore the said letters patent were void." Again,

King Henry VI granted to the company of dyers in London the power to search for cloth dyed with poisonous dyes and to seize and confiscate it, if found. The judges held this also against the law of the land on the ground that no one's property could be forfeited by virtue of letters patent without adjudication and an opportunity to be heard. There is a long succession of these cases between the reigns of Henry IV and Elizabeth in which the crown is manifestly endeavoring to make the royal power to protect social interests a source of revenue or a means of enriching favorites, while the courts insist it shall be exercised according to settled principles of reason and within limits defined by the law. To this extent the common law was struggling with the prerogatives of the crown precisely as today it struggles with the prerogatives of majorities and pluralities. There is, however, a significant difference. In these contests between courts and crown prior to the Stuarts, the courts had been guarding social interests by preventing perversion to quite different uses of powers which could be used rightfully only to further public or social interests. In the nineteenth century we find common-law courts going much beyond this and thinking themselves bound to put limits in the interest of the individual to social control for the social interest. This change in the spirit of the common law resulted from the political phase of the contests between courts and crown under the Tudors and Stuarts and from the political and juristic theories of the eighteenth century.

It is probable that the further extension of the legal doctrine of supremacy of law has its juristic origin in the medieval conception of the distinction between temporal and spiritual jurisdiction and the entire incompetency of temporal power in the domain of the spiritual. This proposition was so fundamental that medieval judges no doubt thought of temporal administrative or legislative acts which sought to invade the field set apart for the church much as judges of today might regard the statute sarcastically proposed by an English conveyancer—"Be it enacted that during the month of April of each year the King's loyal subjects shall be at liberty to and are hereby enabled to go forth without umbrellas upon any and all public streets, roads and highways without getting wet." Accordingly in the reign of Henry VII a majority of the Court of Common Pleas laid down unhesitatingly that an act of Parliament for seizing the lands of alien monasteries into the king's hands could not make the king a parson. No temporal act, they said, can make the king parson without the assent of the head of the church. In other words, there was a fundamental law, dividing temporal power from spiritual power, which ran back of all states and of all human authority, and even acts of parliament, if they ran counter to this fundamental law, must be disregarded. When at the Reformation the temporal power became supreme, decisions of this sort seemed to sanction a doctrine that the sovereign, whether king or parliament or people, was bound to act within certain limits imposed upon all government by fundamental principles of right and reason which it was beyond the power of lawmakers to change. Such was the legal situation when a new movement in English polity required the common law to fight for its life and gave a political significance to its power of judging of the validity of royal acts and determining whether they were in truth acts of the sovereign.

In the middle of the sixteenth century the common-law courts, struggling to meet the wants of England of the Reformation by a feudal property law and a criminal law devised primarily as a substitute for the rough and ready justice of an outraged neighborhood in the days when self help was the staple remedy, found themselves in a position very like that of American courts, developed in and for the pioneer or agricultural societies of the first half of the nineteenth century which are struggling to meet the wants of today with the rules and the machinery devised for such communities. Moreover, an era of liberalization was at hand. The preceding period, a period of strict law, had regarded only conformity to the letter of the law and compliance with prescribed form. The stage of equity and natural law was at hand, a stage which involved an infusion of morality—an infusion of purely moral ideas developed outside of the legal system. Such periods of liberalization, in which the law is made over by reception of ideas from without, have always involved for a time a movement away from law, a temporary reversion to justice without law. In such periods at first the chief reliance for obtaining justice seems to be the power of the magistrate.

And arbitrary power is looked upon complacently since it is taken to be the sole means of escape from the bonds imposed by the strict law. Thus in the United States today, in a period of legal development which has much in common with the one we are considering, a movement for liberalization, an infusion into the law of ideas developed in the social sciences, has led to a tendency away from courts and law and a reversion to justice without law in the form of revival of executive and even of legislative justice and reliance upon arbitrary governmental power.

Accordingly, in the middle of the sixteenth century lawyers began to complain that the common law was being set aside. Very little business of importance came longer to the king's courts of law. The courts, which for three hundred years had been shaping the law and holding even the king to the limits prescribed thereby, seemed to be losing their hold. The law seemed to be fashioning in quite another type of tribunal and by other hands than those of common-law lawyers. "In criminal causes that were of any political importance," Maitland tells us, "an examination by two or three doctors of the civil law threatened to become a normal part of our procedure." The living law seemed to be making and applying in the King's Council, in the Star Chamber, in the Court of Requests and in the Court of Chancery—all of them courts of a Roman, and, what was more important, a summary procedure. It seemed that judicial justice, administered in courts, was to be superseded by executive justice administered in administrative tribunals or by administrative officers. In other words there was a reaction from justice according to law to justice without law, in this respect entirely parallel to the present movement away from the common-law courts in the United States. In place of the magistrate limited by law and held to walk strictly in the paths fixed by the custom of the realm, men sought to set up a benevolent guardian of social interests who should have power to do freely whatever in his judgment protection of those interests might involve; in place of deliberate judicial tribunals, restrained by formal procedure and deciding according to fixed principles, they turned to offhand administrative tribunals in which the relations of individuals with each other and with the state were adjusted summarily according to the notions for the time being of an administrative officer as to what the general interest or good conscience demanded, unencumbered by many rules.

A valiant fight against this movement for administrative absolutism was waged by the common-law courts, and in the end the older law prevailed. The Court of Chancery was the only one of the Romanized courts of the Tudors and Stuarts which survived and that tribunal little by little was made over along common-law lines till it became an ordinary English court. Moreover the doctrines which were evolved in the course of judicial administration by these tribunals were made into law and received into the common-law system. The law was liberalized but it was still the common law. The chief weapon which the common law employed in this contest and the one about which the contest raged, was the doctrine of the supremacy of law. That doctrine, therefore, became established among the fundamenta of our legal tradition as a result of the victory. But the victory gave it a new scope and a new spirit. Its scope for a time broadened, so as to make of it a doctrine of limitations upon all sovereign power, independent of positive law and at most simply declared thereby. Its spirit became individualist. It became a doctrine that it was the function of the common law and of common-law courts to stand between the individual and oppressive action by the state; that the courts were set up and the law existed to guard individual interests against the encroachments of state and of society. Thus the Sunday-morning conference between King James and the judges, which is the glory of our legal history, led in the nineteenth century to constitutional doctrines that for a time enabled a fortified monopoly to shake its fist in the face of a people and defy investigation or regulation. Too often it led the law in the last century to stand full-armored before individuals, natural and artificial, that needed no defence, but sallied from beneath its aegis to injure society.

Both the broadening of scope and the change of spirit demand notice.

It has been noted already that in the reign of Henry VII the courts had enforced against an act of Parliament the medieval dogma of the distinction between temporal and spiritual jurisdiction. To Coke, the champion of the common law in the contest with the Stuarts, such decisions established a general doctrine of the competence of the courts, since they administered the law and law was reason, to compel not merely all private individuals, and all agents of government, but the very sovereign itself, to keep within the bounds of reason, by refusing to recognize or give legal effect to acts or ordinances of the sovereign which went beyond such bounds. "When an act of Parliament," he said boldly, "is against common right and reason . . . the common law will control it and adjudge such act to be void." The events of 1688 in England established the supremacy of Parliament and Coke's proposition failed to maintain itself. But experience of review of colonial legislation with respect to its conformity to charters, applied to written constitutions and bills of rights, led us in the United States to carry the supremacy of law to its logical limits, and indeed to go beyond such limits and practically adopt Coke's conception of a control of legislation upon fundamental principles of right and reason. Eighteenth-century ideas of natural law and the assumption that the seventeenth-century legal rights of Englishmen were the same as the natural rights of man which were the staple of juristic and political thought in the eighteenth century, combined to give Coke's theory of the supremacy of law much currency. When our courts first came to pass upon constitutional questions, what they read in Coke's Second Institute and in his report of *Bonham's Case* appeared but a common-law version of what they read in French and Dutch publicists as to an eternal and immutable natural law, by which all human laws must be measured, and of which, in order to have validity, they must be declaratory. Accordingly it became usual to speak of limitations involved in the very idea of free government which go back of and are only declared by constitutions and bills of rights. It became usual to think, not of the text of the bills of rights, but of these supposed fundamental principles of which they were but declaratory. Thus unwittingly at the end of the nineteenth century courts found themselves too often enforcing not the bills of rights but the individualist doctrines of the historical and philosophical jurisprudence and classical economics of that century.

Moreover, for reasons in part growing out of the seventeenth-century contests between courts and crown and in part growing out of eighteenth-century political theory, as has been said, this doctrine of a fundamental law, binding even the sovereign, was taken to be something which existed for individuals to protect them against state and society. Assuming that the abstract individual was the center of all things and that the state existed only to secure his interests, it was thought that courts and law had for their function to prevent use of this machinery, set up to protect the individual and to secure his rights, as a means of oppressing him and depriving him of his rights. To understand this notion, as it developed in the Anglo-American juristic tradition, we must look for a moment at the history of the idea of sovereignty.

In the Roman polity the power of making laws was in the *populus Romanus*. The magistrate had *imperium,* the power to command the citizens; a name and an idea growing out of the combined civic and military functions of the magistrate in the ancient city-state. To protect society by keeping discipline in time of war and by keeping order in time of peace, the magistrate had a power of command. Later the emperor had delegated to him both of these powers. The people conferred on him their legislative power for life and they made him magistrate for life. Thus arose in the Byzantine period the conception of a sovereign in whom all the law-making and all the coercive powers of organized political society are concentrated, and this conception was handed down to the modern world in the law books of Justinian.

Imperium and *dominium,* the power of the magistrate and the power of the owner, were confused during the Middle Ages. The great land owner was also a territorial ruler; the owner of the manor was also magistrate and judge within its limits. The king was ultimate lord of the soil and also the fountain of justice. Under the reign of the Germanic idea of reciprocal rights and duties involved in such a relation the royal *dominium* was more like *imperium* than the sovereignty of the Byzantine texts. But the breakdown of feudalism, the growth of central national authority in place of the local feudal lordships, and the rise of the nationalist idea at the Reformation, with the accompanying notion of the duty of passive obedience to rulers, gave significance to these texts as a more scientific study of Roman law went forward as a result of the Renaissance and of the humanist movement. In France, where the treatises of widest influence were written, there was coming to be something very like the Byzantine *princeps,* and in England if Tudor and Stuart had had their way there would have been a like result. Throughout western Europe the idea of sovereignty as a control from without, of the sovereign as something external to society and set over it, something with which the several individuals who compose society had made a compact binding them to obedience or to which as of divine right passive obedience was due—throughout western Europe this idea superseded the Germanic and feudal conception of a relation of protection and service growing out of tenure of land and involving reciprocal rights and duties. When this idea came to prevail the sovereign was a Byzantine emperor. What it willed had the force of law. Law was not something fundamental and eternal, running back of all states, it was the will of this state or that; the command of this or that sovereign. Whatever the moral duties of sovereigns, they were incapable of legal limitation. They might rule under God, but they certainly did not and could not rule under the law, for they made the law. This conception of law as will has been struggling with the idea of law as reason ever since.

When the common law, with its feudal theory of the relation of king and subject and its Germanic theory of the supremacy of law came in conflict with the new conception of sovereignty developed in France on Byzantine lines, it was forced to a position which seemed in practice to assert that the sovereign had legal duties to the subjects, that there was law above and behind all sovereigns which they could not alter and by which their actions might be judged, and that the law stood between the individual subject or citizen and this leviathan and compelled it to recognize the natural rights of the individual, given him by this eternal and immutable law, or to recognize the terms of the social compact whereby the individual had conferred upon leviathan his very sovereignty and the latter in return had undertaken to secure those natural rights. At the Revolution, the peoples of the several states succeeded to the sovereignty of Parliament. They thought of this not as feudal but as Byzantine sovereignty. And yet they were afraid and justly afraid of these emperors they were setting over themselves, even though the *princeps* was a fluctuating body made up of a majority or plurality of themselves. Hence by bills of rights they sought to impose legal limits upon the action of those who wielded the powers of sovereignty, while adhering to a political theory of illimitable and uncontrollable power in the sovereign itself. It was inevitable that this compromise between inconsistent theories should sooner or later produce a conflict between courts and people. In that conflict, which became acute in the first decade of the present century, each was in a measure right and each was in a measure wrong.

"Talk of stubborn facts," says Dr. Crothers, "they are but babes beside a stubborn theory." The conflict between courts and people was not a contest of theory with fact. It was a conflict of two stubborn theories. It was a conflict of juristic theory with political theory as to what law is, whence it comes and whence it derives its force. Each theory was the outgrowth of the law and politics of the seventeenth and eighteenth centuries. I shall have to say more as to this conflict in my next lecture. Suffice it to say here that if, as I shall try to show on another occasion, the classical juristic theory as laid down by Coke and developed in the eighteenth century is untenable and must be abandoned by the jurist, the classical political theory as laid down by the sixteenth- and seventeenth-century publicists and developed in the eighteenth century in an age of absolute governments, must likewise be abandoned. Indeed the French who have advocated it most zealously and given it the furthest logical development are now beginning to throw it over and are urging that sovereignty is not force from without but is public service from within. Properly understood, and shorn of the extravagances that it acquired through seventeenth- and eighteenth-century theories of natural law, the doctrine of supremacy of law is entirely in accord with such a conception. Public service, whether by a railroad company or by a municipal corporation or by the state, is not an end but a means. In neither case may it be left to the arbitrary will of those who perform it. In each case the social interest in general security requires that it be guided and regulated by reason; that it conform to principles and standards formulated dispassionately in advance of controversy upon weighing of all the interests to be affected. In insisting on the supremacy of law, the common law is not bound of necessity to stand always against the popular will in the interest of the abstract individual. Rather its true position is one of standing for ultimate and more important social interests as against the more immediately pressing but less weighty interests of the moment by which mere will unrestrained by reason is too likely to be swayed.

I have made more than one comparison between the period of the Tudor and Stuart kings, in which the contests between courts and crown shaped our doctrine of the supremacy of the law, and the present period, in which contests between courts and majorities or pluralities have threatened to overthrow it. One more remains to be made which is by no means the least significant. At the very time that absolute ideas of lawmaking were dominant through the rise of the absolute theory of sovereignty and acceptance of the Byzantine doctrine that the will of the emperor has the force of law, a period of juridical idealism was at hand which proceeded upon a radically different idea. Our law and the law of Continental Europe were liberalized and modernized in the seventeenth and eighteenth centuries, not by legislation, not by exercise of the will of any sovereign, but by a juristic doctrine that all legal institutions and all legal rules were to be measured by reason and that nothing could stand in law that could not maintain itself in reason. So today, while absolute theories of law as a mere expression of the popular will are current in political thinking, a return to juridical idealism is in progress. Once more jurists of Continental Europe are writing elaborate treatises on natural law. In the United States, a revival of philosophical jurisprudence has definitely begun and conscious attempt to make the law conform to ideals is once more becoming the creed of jurisprudence.

This does not mean that jurists are going back to the eighteenth-century conception of a set of fundamental legal principles of universal validity for all men, in all places, in all times, from which a complete set of rules might be drawn by purely logical processes. They are content to search for the ideals of the age and to set them up as a guide. They are content to seek what Kohler calls the jural postulates of the civilization of the time. But they are not content to abdicate all function and to concede that court and lawyer have no more to do than to ascertain and interpret the will of the majority or plurality for the time being. The notion of juristic superfluity involved in such a doctrine is as impossible in the complex industrial society of today as the notion of legislative futility, held so generally during the hegemony of the historical school, or the notion of juristic futility added thereto by the positivists. Men are not born with intuitions of the principles by which justice may be attained through the public adjudication of controversies. The administration of justice is not an easy task to which every man is competent. It is no more possible for the people to administer justice directly or to control the course of justice directly than it is for them to administer medicine or control the course of medical science directly or to direct armies and control the course of military science. In each case, study of the experience of the past joined with scientific understanding of the problems involved is the road to the ends sought, and a technical body of knowledge inevitably results which may be mastered only through special study and training. Such was the element of truth in Coke's answer to his sovereign. Indeed every attempt in legal history to go back to justice without law has enforced the lesson which the judges of England sought to impress upon King James at their Sunday conference. In this country we should have learned it when, in the period after the Revolution, the bitter hostility to lawyers and the attempt ruthlessly to break down the professional tradition, to insure the access of the untrained and incompetent to the opportunities of the bar and to degrade the judicial office, resulted only in establishing the lawyer as the leader of the community and in intrenching the fundamental dogmas of the common law in our constitutions.

We may be assured, therefore, that the supremacy of law, established by the common law against Tudor and Stuart is not to disappear. We may be confident that we shall have, not merely laws, expressions of the popular will for the time being, but law, an expression of reason applied to the relations of man with man and of man with the state. We may be confident also that in the new period of legal development which is at hand as in like periods in legal history there will be a working over of the jural materials of the past and working into them of new ideas from without. We shall be warranted in prophesying that this working over will be effected by means of a philosophical theory of right and justice and conscious attempt to make the law conform to ideals. Such a period will be a period of scientific law, made, if not by judges, then by lawyers trained in the universities; not one of arbitrary law based on the fiat of any sovereign, however hydra-headed. For the notion of law as the will of the people belongs to the past era of a complete and stable system in which certainty and security were the sole ends. Throughout legal history law has been stagnant whenever the imperative idea has been uppermost. Law has lived and grown through juristic activity. It has been liberalized by ideas of natural right or justice or reasonableness or utility, leading to criteria by which rules and principles and standards might be tested, not by ideas of force and command and the sovereign will as the ultimate source of authority. Attempts to reduce the judicial office in the United States to the purely mechanical function of applying rules imposed from without and of serving as a mouthpiece for the popular will for the moment are not in the line of progress.

IV

THE RIGHTS OF ENGLISHMEN AND THE RIGHTS OF MAN

IN PRIMITIVE law the end is simply to keep the peace. The legal order is a peaceable order at whatever cost, and in consequence whatever serves to avert private vengeance and prevent private war is an instrument of justice. In its beginning law is no more than a body of rules by which controversies are adjusted peaceably. At first, therefore, it attempts nothing more than to furnish the injured a substitute for revenge. Where modern law thinks of compensation for an injury, primitive law thought of composition for the desire to be avenged. Thus the original Roman law dealt with injury to the person under the head of insult; the earliest of the Anglo-Saxon laws provided two-fold payment where a bruise was not covered by the clothes and so subjected the victim to chaffing and increased his desire to be revenged; the Salic law gave double composition to the Frank, accustomed to right his own wrongs, as compared with the Roman, trained for generations to adjust his controversies in court.

Greek philosophy and Roman law soon got beyond the crude conception of primitive law and gave us in its place an idea of the legal order as a device to preserve the social *status quo;* to keep each man in his appointed groove and thus prevent the friction with his fellows which the older conception sought only to mitigate. Thus in Plato's ideal state every member of the community is to be assigned to the class for which he proves to be best fitted; then the law is to keep him there and so, it was conceived, "a perfect harmony and unity will characterize both the state and every person in it." To Aristotle also, rights, that is interests to be protected by law, existed only between those who were free and equal. The law was in the first instance to take account of relations of inequality in which individuals were treated according to their worth. Then, each being in his proper place, the law would keep him there and would preserve among equals a unanimity in which there would be no violation of mutual rights. The well-known exhortation in which St. Paul calls upon everyone to exert himself to do his duty in the class in which he finds himself, brings out this same idea.

Roman legal genius gave practical effect to this conception of justice as a preservation of the social *status quo* by conceiving it to be the province of the state to define and protect the interests and powers of action which in their aggregate make up the legal personality of the individual. As laid down in the Institutes of Justinian, the precepts of law are three: to live honorably, not to injure another, to give to everyone his due. What the interests of another are which one is not to injure, what constitutes anyone's due which is to be given him, are questions left to the traditional and authoritative social organization. In other words, we have here the Greek idea of the end of the legal system, the idea that it exists to maintain harmoniously the existing social order.

In the Middle Ages Germanic law brought back for a time the primitive conception of merely keeping the peace and the primitive institutions of buying off vengeance, of a tariff of compositions and of private war. But as the authority of Justinian in law and of Aristotle in philosophy came to be accepted, this conception of justice gave way to the classical idea of preservation of the social *status quo,* which, indeed, had behind it not merely Aristotle and the Roman law but the unassailable authority of more than one text of Scripture. Hence in the Middle Ages, as in Antiquity, the idea of a device to keep the peace is succeeded by the idea of a device to maintain the social *status quo.* This conception of the end of law was not questioned till the Reformation. Then the appeal to reason against authority led to a new conception in philosophy, in theology, in politics and ultimately in legal theory, as a result of which the legal order came to be thought of as a device to secure a maximum of individual self-assertion. The beginnings of the change are in philosophy, in the attempt to sustain authority by reason. But the Middle Ages added nothing to the juristic theory of the end of law and only prepared the way, through philosophy, for the new conception which developed in the seventeenth century.

We commonly fix the date of the new era in jurisprudence by the appearance of the great work of

Grotius in 1625. As he and those who followed him expounded the new doctrine it had two sides. On the one hand there was a theory of limitations upon human activities imposed by reason in view of human nature, on the other hand there was a theory of moral qualities inherent in human beings, or natural rights, demonstrated by reason as deductions from human nature. The first had been worked out by those who went before Grotius, especially the Spanish jurist-theologians of the preceding century. They had sought to combine the newer ideas of the political order with the older ideas of the unity of law as eternal verity rather than state enactment. Accordingly in developing the conception of unity of the law as a universal and eternal body of principles, they thought of restraints upon states, of certain limits to their activities which they could not overpass, so that in international law there were limits of state activity in the relations of states with other states, in political theory there were limits of state activity in the relations of state to subject, in juristic theory there were limits of individual activity in the relations of individuals with each other. Grotius, and seventeenth-century jurisprudence following him, made reason the measure of all obligation. Thus at the very time that the common law had established its doctrine of supremacy of law and had turned the feudal duties of the paramount lord toward his tenants into legal duties of the king toward his subjects, a juristic theory of fundamental limitations upon the activities of states, of rulers and of individuals dictated by eternal reason, had sprung up independently to furnish the scientific explanation.

As has been said, Grotius and those who followed him made reason the measure of all obligation. They conceived that the end for which law exists is to produce conformity to the nature of rational creatures. They had broken with authority as authority, but they accepted the Roman law as embodied reason and ventured little that did not have authority behind it. Hence they accepted the Roman maxim—not to injure another and to give to everyone his due, that is, respect for personality and respect for acquired rights—as conformity to the nature of rational creatures. This raised certain obvious problems: What is injury to another? What is there in personality that makes aggression an injury? What is it that constitutes anything one's own? Grotius and his successors tried to answer by a theory of natural rights; not merely natural law, as before, not merely principles of eternal validity, but certain qualities inherent in persons and demonstrated by reason and recognized by natural law, to which therefore the national law ought to give effect. Thus, again, at the very time that the victory of the courts in the contests between the common-law courts and the Stuart kings had established that there were fundamental common-law rights of Englishmen which Englishmen might maintain in courts and in which courts would secure them even against the king, a juristic theory of fundamental natural rights, independent of and running back of all states, which states might secure and ought to secure, but could not alter or abridge, had sprung up independently and was at hand to furnish a scientific explanation when the next century called for one. By a natural transition, the common-law limitations upon royal authority became natural limitations upon all authority; the common-law rights of Englishmen became the natural rights of man. Each underwent some change of substance along with this change of name.

To understand this change and the effect which it had upon the law as we received it at the end of the eighteenth century and worked it over in the fore part of the nineteenth century, we must examine the theory of natural rights, the theory of the relation of law to natural rights, and the theory of natural law and of the possibility of deducing a fixed and complete system of positive law from the principles of natural law, as these theories were held when our bills of rights were framed and our constitutional law was formative.

According to the Grotian definition, a right is "that quality in a person which makes it just or right for him either to possess certain things or to do certain actions." The medieval idea was that law existed to maintain those powers of control over things and those powers of action which the social system had awarded or attributed to each man. The Grotian idea was that law exists to maintain and give effect to certain inherent moral qualities in every man which reason discovers for us, by virtue of which he ought to have certain powers of control over things or certain powers of action.

But one of the characteristics of the stage of liberalization which may be called the stage of equity or natural law is a tendency to hold that the legal and the moral are necessarily synonymous, that if something ought to be juristically, for that reason alone it is legally. Hence the scheme of natural rights that the law ought to secure, quickly becomes the scheme of fundamental rights which it does secure, legal rights being taken to be merely declaratory thereof.

There was a good side to all this. The insistence on what ought to be as the measure of what is did no less than create international law, and it liberalized and modernized the actual law of the European states through the juristic testing of every doctrine and every category with reference to its basis in reason. But it had a bad side. It led to a confusion between the interests which it is conceived the law ought to recognize and the rights by which the law secures interests when recognized, which has been the bane of jurisprudence ever since, and it led to absolute notions of an ideal development of received legal ideas as the jural order of nature which later brought legal thought and popular political thought into an obstinate conflict.

A legal system attains its end by recognizing certain interests, individual, public and social; by defining the limits within which these interests shall be recognized legally and given effect through the force of the state, and by endeavoring to secure the interests so recognized within the defined limits. It does not create these interests. There is so much truth in the eighteenth-century theory of natural rights. Undoubtedly the progress of society and the development of government increase the number and variety of these interests. But they arise, apart from the law, through the competition of individuals with each other, the competition of groups or societies with each other and the competition of individuals with such groups or societies. The law does not create them, it only recognizes them. Yet it does not have for its sole function to recognize interests which exist independently. It must determine which it will recognize, it must define the extent to which it will give effect to them in view of other interests, individual, public or social, and the possibilities of effective interference by law, and it must devise the means by which they shall be secured. Such is the theory of today. The seventeenth- and eighteenth-century theory, however, confused the interest, which exists independently of law, and the legal right, the creature of law. It confused the interest, which the law recognizes in whole or in part and seeks to secure, with the right by which the law gives effect to the interest when recognized and to the extent of the recognition. Natural rights mean simply interests which we think ought to be secured; demands which human beings may make which we think ought to be satisfied. It is perfectly true that neither law nor state creates them. But it is fatal to all sound thinking to treat them as legal conceptions. For legal rights, the devices which law employs to secure such of these interests as it is expedient to recognize, are the work of the law and in that sense the work of the state. Through the exaltation of individual interests which resulted from the theory of natural rights and the confusion of interest and legal right involved therein, the natural rights of men presently became as tyrannous as the divine rights of states and rulers.

It soon became apparent that the theory of inherent moral qualities, while it would serve for interests of personality—for claims to be secure in one's body and life and the interests immediately related thereto—would not serve as a basis for the so-called natural right of property—for the *suum cuique* element of justice, or, as we put it today, for interests of substance. None of the jurists of that time questioned the existing social order. On the contrary they assumed as beyond question a natural right of property. They conceived that security of acquisitions, including what one had acquired through the existing social order, was a chief end. At the same time they could not but see a difference between this natural right and such rights as those to the integrity of one's body, to free motion and locomotion and to free speech. Accordingly jurists turned for an explanation to the idea of contract.

It must be remembered that contract in this connection has reference to the Roman conception of a legal transaction, an act intended to have legal consequences to which the law attributes the intended result. In the seventeenth and eighteenth centuries this was the staple legal analogy. The idea of the legal transaction was the most important contribution of Rome to the law, and in an age when trade and commerce were expanding the law of such transactions was becoming the living part of the legal system. The juristic problem of the time was to reconcile the needs of business and the ethical ideas of good faith which accompanied the infusion of morals into the law with the traditional categories of contracts in Roman law. Naturally contract loomed large in juristic thought for two centuries. Moreover, the central point in the theory of the legal transaction is will, the will to produce a possible and legally permissible result. But the central idea in the theory of natural law and of natural rights was conformity to the nature of reasoning creatures possessed of wills. So the question, how could such creatures acquire rights against one another seemed easy to answer. How, indeed, could this be except by contract; through a legal transaction? Thus the foundation of the natural rights, which the law existed to maintain, was taken to be a legal transaction, a compact of all men with all men by virtue of which rights and corresponding duties were created. Justice, therefore, consisted in respecting and observing the terms of this compact and the business of the jurist and the lawmaker was to discover and to interpret its terms. The sole end of the law was taken to be a giving effect to the inherent moral qualities in individual men, whereby things are theirs, or a securing to individual men of those things to which they are entitled under the terms of the social compact.

Not only was the eighteenth-century system of natural rights a closed hard and fast system, for the jurists of that time were sure that they could deduce all the terms of the social compact and all the inherent moral qualities of mankind from the nature of man in the abstract, but the eighteenth-century theory of law was no less absolute. It was conceived that there were first principles of law inherent in nature and that these principles were discoverable by deduction as necessary results of human nature. Hence it was thought possible to discover, and that the jurists had discovered, principles of universal validity, among all men, in all places and in all times from which might be deduced a complete code for the lawgiver, a complete constitution for the statesman and an infallible guide to the conscience for the individual. It was thought possible through elaborate bills of rights to prescribe universal principles by which legislation might be guided for all time.

Identification of the common-law rights of Englishmen with the natural rights of man and of the fundamental law for which Coke contended with the immutable and eternal natural law had two consequences for our common-law tradition. One was to give currency to an idea of the finality of the common law. For, as has always been true when men have believed in absolute theories of the sort, the principles, supposed to be the dictates of nature, flowed in practice from one of two sources. On social, economic and ethical questions, nature was always found to dictate the personal views of the individual jurist as they had been fixed and settled by education, association and, perhaps, class interest. On legal questions, nature was found to dictate for the most part the principles of law with which the individual jurist was familiar and under which he had grown up. Just as in nine cases out of ten natural law meant for the Continental jurist of the seventeenth and eighteenth centuries an ideal development of the principles of the Roman law, which he knew and had studied, for the common-law lawyer it came to mean an ideal development of the common law. The past generation of lawyers brought up on Blackstone, learned this mode of thinking as part of the rudiments of legal education. More recently our historical legal scholarship, assuming that all of our legal system was at least implicit in the law reports of the sixteenth and seventeenth centuries, if not in the Year Books, gave us a natural law upon historical premises. Hence scholar and lawyer concurred in what became a thorough-going conviction of the nineteenth century, that at least the principal dogmas of the common law were of universal validity and were established by nature. When the lawyer spoke of law he thought of these doctrines. He conceived that constitutions and bills of rights simply declared them. He construed statutes into accord with them. He forced them upon modern social legislation. When he reminded the sovereign people that it ruled under God and the law, he meant that these doctrines, which he conceived as going back of all constitutions and beyond the reach of legislation, were to be the measure of state activity. This was not the true common law. The common law rested on the idea that reason not arbitrary will should be the measure of action and of decision. But the eighteenth century was sure that it had the one key to reason and was fond of laying out philosophical and political and legal charts by which men were to be guided for all time.

Examples of this idea of the finality of the common law and of the identity of its principles with the principles of natural law may be found throughout the reports of the last century. Thus in the great case of *Fletcher* v. *Peck,* where a statute of Georgia revoking a land grant on the ground that it had been procured by fraud was in question, it appeared that the land had passed into the hands of a purchaser for value without notice. This being so, Chief Justice Marshall said that, apart from particular provisions in the federal constitution, the state was restrained from such legislation by "general principles which are common to our free institutions." The general principle here was the familiar one that equity will not set aside a transaction for fraud where the title to what was parted with through fraud has passed to a purchaser for value without notice. This principle depends upon the history of our courts of equity and the relation of equity to law in our system. Apart from this history, it has not seemed so intrinsically self-evident to recent thinkers. In the same spirit, at the end of the century, when legislation prohibiting employees from making certain contracts came before the courts we find more than one laying down a doctrine of natural incapacities to which the legislature is incompetent to add new ones based merely on the facts of modern industrial employment. In the event these "natural incapacities" all prove to be incapacities which were recognized at common law. In the same spirit, in the present century we find an able court saying of the fellow-servant rule that it "is a part of the general American common law, resting upon considerations of right and justice." The fundamental conceptions of our traditional case law came to be regarded as fundamental conceptions of legal science. Not merely the jurist, but the legislator, the sociologist, the criminologist, the labor leader, and in the case of our corporation laws and laws as to restraint of trade the business man had to reckon with them. With the coming of a period of collectivist thinking and of social legislation, conflict was inevitable.

Such a conflict did result when the absolute theory of law came in contact with an equally absolute theory of politics. While on the one hand the legal theory as to the nature of law had become absolute through the general acceptance of the eighteenth-century conception, a political theory became established on the other hand which ran counter to the whole common-law theory of law and of lawmaking. For the popular theory of sovereignty, what we may call the classical American political theory, is quite as firmly rooted in the mind of the public as the eighteenth-century theory of law is rooted in the mind of the lawyer. The layman is taught this political theory in school, he reads it in the newspapers, he listens to it on the Fourth of July and from the stump and from Chautauqua platforms, and he seldom or never hears it questioned. In consequence, he is as thoroughly sure of it as is the lawyer of his juristic theory. If the lawyer is moved to stigmatize all that does not comport with his doctrine as lawlessness, the people at large are moved to stigmatize all that does not comport with their theory as usurpation.

While the lawyer as a rule still believes that the principles of law are absolute, eternal, and of universal validity, and that law is found, not made, the people believe no less firmly that it may be made and that they have the power to make it. While to the lawyer the state enforces law because it is law, to the people law is law because the state, reflecting their desires, has so willed. While to the lawyer law is above and beyond all will, to the people it is but the formulation of the general will. Hence it often happens that when the lawyer thinks he is enforcing the law, the people think he is overturning the law. While, for example, the lawyer thinks of popular action as subject to legal limitations running back of all constitutions and merely reasserted, not created, thereby, the people think of themselves as the authors of all constitutions and limitations and the final judges of their meaning and effect. This conflict between the lawyer's theory and the political theory weakens the force of law. The lawyer's theory leads him to pay scant attention to legislation or to mold it and warp it to the exigencies of what he regards as the real law. But to those who do not share his theory, this appears as a high-handed over-riding of law, and the layman, laboring under that impression, is unable to perceive why the lawyers should have a monopoly of that convenient power. On the other hand, the people's theory that law is wholly a conscious product of the human will tends to produce arbitrary and ill-considered legislation impossible of satisfactory application to actual controversies. Each of these absolute theories must be given up.

A second effect of eighteenth-century theory upon the common-law tradition was to intensify the individualism of which for other reasons it had quite enough. In both its aspects the juristic theory of natural rights was thoroughly individualist. As a theory of inherent moral qualities of persons, it was based on deduction from the nature of an abstract isolated individual. As a theory of rights based upon a social compact, it thought of natural rights as the rights of individuals who had entered into a contract, apart from which there would and could be no law and nothing for the law to maintain. In either view, the law exists to maintain and protect individual interests. This fitted the legal theory of the common-law rights of Englishmen so perfectly that there is no cause for wonder that the founders of our political and legal and judicial systems, who were studying Coke and Blackstone on the one hand and the French and Dutch publicists on the other, thought they were reading about the same things. Hence Americans of the end of the eighteenth century argued for either or for both. The declaration of rights of the Continental Congress of 1774 asserted the legal rights of Englishmen. The Declaration of Independence of 1776 asserted the natural rights of man. Yet each claimed essentially the same things. It followed that the common law was taken to be a system of giving effect to individual natural rights. It was taken to exist in order to secure individual interests, not merely against aggression by other individuals, but even more against arbitrary invasion by state or society. It followed also that the bills of rights, declaratory of natural rights, were likewise declaratory of the common law. This idea is very prominent in judicial discussions of liberty of contract in the nineteenth century. For example, one court in passing on legislation directed against fines in cotton mills, tells us that a statute which violates "fundamental rights" is unconstitutional and void even though the enactment of it is not expressly forbidden. Another court tells us that natural persons do not derive their right to contract from the law. Hence whatever the state may do in limiting the power of a corporation to make certain contracts, because the corporation gets its power from the state, it may not limit the contractual capacity of natural persons, who got their power to contract from nature, so that nature alone may remove it. Another court, in passing adversely upon legislation against company stores, said that any classification was arbitrary and unconstitutional, unless it proceeded on the "natural capacity of persons to contract." Another, in passing on a similar statute denied that contractual capacity may be restricted except for physical or mental disabilities. Another held that the legislature could not take notice of the de facto subjection of one class of persons to another in making contracts of employment in certain industries, but must be governed by the theoretical jural equality. All these instances come to the proposition that the common-law categories of disability are final and that legislation may not add new ones. The bills of rights and the Fourteenth Amendment were treated as but declaring a natural liberty which was also a common-law liberty; hence an abridgement not known to the common law was thought to go counter to their fair construction, if not to their letter.

Perhaps nothing contributed so much to create and foster the hostility to courts and law and constitutions, which was conspicuous at the end of the nineteenth century and at the beginning of the present century, as this conception of the courts as guardians of individual natural rights against the state and against society, of the law as a final and absolute body of doctrine declaring these individual natural rights, and of constitutions as declaratory of common-law principles, which are also natural-law principles, anterior to the state and of superior validity to enactments by the authority of the state, having for their purpose to guarantee and maintain the natural rights of individuals against society and all its agencies. When houses are scarce and landlords are grasping, Blackstone's proposition that the public good is in nothing more essentially interested than in the protection of every individual's private rights is not the popular view. A crowded, urban, industrial community looks to society for protection against predatory individuals, natural or artificial, and resents doctrines that protect these individuals against society for fear society will oppress them. But the common-law guarantees of individual rights are established in our constitutions, state and federal. So that, while in England these common-law dogmas have had to give way to modern legislation, in America they have stood continually between the people, or large classes of the people, and legislation they desire. In consequence, the courts were long put in a false position of doing nothing and obstructing everything, which it was impossible for the layman to interpret aright.

It is not in constitutional law alone that the common-law rights of Englishmen, translated into rights of man and intrenched in constitutions, have been a source of popular irritation toward the law. American criminal procedure has done scarcely less to produce discontent with judicial administration of justice. But judicial administration of punitive justice is hedged about on every side with constitutional guarantees securing the so-called natural rights of the accused. All crimes of any consequence were once felonies punishable with death. The reform that led to milder sentences and more humane punishments came after the principles and even the detailed rules of criminal procedure had been well established. The judges "favoring life in capital cases," and all cases of any consequence were capital, "took advantage of the slightest technical defect to discharge a defendant, and form became in the highest degree essential." When the common-law rights of the accused Englishman became the natural rights of the accused man and these rights were intrenched in state and federal constitutions, these rules and the spirit in which they were conceived were projected into a time in which they were not merely inapplicable but downright harmful. Bentham long ago pointed out the ill effects of the complicated, expensive and time-consuming machinery of a common-law criminal prosecution. Many states, however, guarantee to an accused the power to insist upon all of this wasteful machinery as a natural right which legislation must hold sacred. Again, another serious defect in our criminal procedure is the lack of any legal mode of interrogating the accused. In practice the rich malefactor takes the advice of counsel, closes his mouth and leaves the prosecution to prove what it may. The police labor with the friendless malefactor till a confession is extorted. Let us note how the privilege of the accused against interrogation and the rules of evidence as to confessions arose. When these institutions of the law grew up, petty offences against property were felonies and the offenders were peasants and laborers, habituated by generations of subordination to an exaggerated, one may say a stupid, deference to authority. As Dean Wigmore has said, in commenting upon the rules as to confessions, "the situation of such a peasant, charged by his landlord with poaching and urged to confess, the situation of a maid urged and threatened by her mistress to confess a petty theft, involves a mental condition to which we may well hesitate to apply the test of a rational principle. We may believe that rationally a false confession is not to be apprehended from a normal person under certain paltry inducements or meaningless threats; but we have here perhaps a person not to be tested by a normal or rational standard." It is not to be wondered at that the judges of a hundred and fifty or even a hundred years ago strained every point to exclude confessions and prevent interrogation of accused persons. But under modern conditions of an emancipated proletariat fully conscious of its rights and filled with scant respect for authority, the whole basis of these rulings has failed, and today the immunity from interrogation and the strict rules as to confessions do the poor no good and are an unnecessary burden upon the prosecutor. Immunity of accused persons from all interrogation, if they are firm, well-advised and able to give bail, is a most effective shield of wrongdoers. Knowledge of this tempts police and detectives and prosecutors to lawless modes of getting what cannot be had lawfully whenever the poor and defenceless are in their custody. Granting all that may be said as to the abuses to which a legal form of interrogation is liable, the fact remains that the present state of the law operates unequally and invites oppression and lawlessness. No rich man has been subjected to the third degree to obtain proof of violation of anti-trust or anti-rebate legislation, and no powerful politician has been so dealt with in order to obtain proof of bribery or graft. The common-law right of the accused poacher, become the natural right of the accused magnate and intrenched in the bill of rights, shows how legal machinery may defeat its own ends when one age conceives it has said the final word and assumes to prescribe unalterable rules for time to come. Lawyers of the last century were brought up on the doctrine of natural rights and the conception that law exists to secure these rights to the individual as against state and society, as fundamental doctrines. They were brought up to believe that the highest social interest was an interest in securing to every one these natural rights. Inevitably they regarded protection of the supposed right of the accused to every jot of procedural advantage afforded him by a ritual born of obsolete conditions as a duty superior to protection from lawlessness, since the first interest of the public lay in maintaining that same right.

Thinking of common-law rights as declaratory of natural rights and of common-law doctrines as declaratory of natural law has led to bad results also in the attitude of courts toward legislation. The courts have done more than enforce their ideas of economics upon reluctant communities in passing upon the constitutionality of social legislation. Through their power of interpretation they have made statutes yield to their juristic ideas in the very teeth of legislative intent. Usually they have done this from belief in the eternal and unalterable character of common-law doctrines and common-law institutions. Conceiving some doctrines to be beyond the reach of legislation, they have held that statutes were meant only to reaffirm and declare these doctrines and not to introduce anything new. Conceiving that case law is the normal type and legislature-made law something exceptional, to be resorted to only on special occasions and for special reasons, they have insisted that we must presume the legislature intended no innovation upon the common law, must construe strictly all departures therefrom, and must restrict the operation of changes to those particulars with respect to which the statute is clear and express. Bearing in mind that the common law thus protected so zealously from all modification is essentially judge-made, these doctrines certainly come very close to a judicial assertion of legislative incompetence to deal with ordinary legal relations. To take another example: If a state legislature acts unreasonably and arbitrarily in the enactment of an oppressive statute, the courts conceive that there is a deprivation of liberty or property within the purview of the Fourteenth Amendment, and the federal courts, if necessary, will refuse to give effect to the enactment or will even restrain its operation. If the state executive acts unreasonably and arbitrarily to the injury of an individual, the same position will be taken; the act is fairly certain to be held of no effect. But let the state judiciary act in the same way, and the divinity that doth hedge about a court requires a different result. If the highest court of a state decides arbitrarily and unreasonably in defiance of all legal principle there is no remedy; the protection which the Fourteenth Amendment throws around liberty and property when they are threatened by legislative or executive action is withdrawn. In such a case our highest federal tribunal will not act. One need not complain of these propositions. It is enough to state them as facts. Whether the doctrines are desirable or undesirable they demonstrate that judges, like the king and like the people, when they act upon absolute theories are not easily confined by self-imposed limitations and may even wield absolute power in an arbitrary manner. Probably of the three they are on the whole least likely to do so. For the training and bent of judges leads them to subordinate everything to principles and general rules. Even when they overstep legal bounds, they do so according to rules and upon a system. Their theory is that some rule or principle contains a better expression of the law. But a theory must be judged by its fruits. One under which so many of our state courts in the last century made of the proposition that statutes will not be held unconstitutional unless their repugnance to the constitution is beyond doubt "a mere courteous and smoothly transmitted platitude" is worse than an anachronism.

But we must not infer that the contribution of eighteenth-century theory to our legal tradition is to be cast out utterly. For the theory of fundamental principles to which law must conform and of fundamental interests which law must secure at all events has another side. Those who held it were willing to do justice and to suffer justice to be done against their immediate interests for the very sake of justice, and they were eager to vindicate justice at any cost. Where the eighteenth-century and the nineteenth-century American were willing to bear a hand in the administration of justice by asserting rights even at a sacrifice, today vindication of right and justice are generally, if not universally, coming to be secondary to the trouble and expense involved. Where the common law relied on individual initiative, we are more and more turning to administrative interference. No doubt the delay and expense in litigation involved in our judicial organization has had much to do with the one phenomenon, and our excessive reliance on individual action and the requirements of large cities, of the relation of employer and employed in modern industry and of distribution in a highly specialized society have had much to do with the latter. But beyond what may be assigned to these causes there has been a marked change. "The administration of justice," said Daniel Webster, "is the great end of human society," and he pronounced justice, meaning the end of the legal order, "the greatest interest of man on earth." In contrast with such statements, which were staple in the last century, men are saying today that material welfare is the great end to which all institutions must be directed and by which they must be measured. Men are not asking merely to be allowed to achieve welfare; they are asking to have welfare achieved for them through organized society. Much that advertises itself as social is in truth individualist; it is individualism to be attained through society rather than through individual self-help. Even though we seek social ends through law, law is not self-enforcing. Except as a vigorous despot may for a time put rules in force by the might of his arms, enforcement depends ultimately upon the general will. And this does not mean an abstract desire that a rule or a body of rules be adhered to. It means a steadfast will on the part of the individual citizen to obey the rule in action and to see to it that others obey it also. An active individual popular interest in justice, a fixed and constant popular determination to secure for everyone his due is a prerequisite of an effective legal system. The law may give effect to this determination. It cannot create it. An easy-going attitude toward right and justice bodes as ill for law as an easy-going attitude toward politics bodes ill for government and administration. The individual citizen must do his duty with respect to the one no less than with respect to the other, if the machinery of the modern state is to be effective.

Moreover, even if we grant that ultimately all interests, individual and public, are secured and maintained because of a social interest in so doing, this does not mean that individual interests, the details of which the last two centuries worked out so thoroughly, are to be ignored. On the contrary the chiefest of social interests is the moral and social life of the individual; and thus individual interests become largely identical with a social interest. Just as in the seventeenth century an undue insistence upon public interests, thought of as the interests of the sovereign, defeated the moral and social life of the individual and required the assertion of individual interests in bills of rights and declarations of rights, there is like danger now that certain social interests will be unduly emphasized and that governmental maternalism will become an end rather than a means and defeat the real purposes of the legal order. Although we think socially, we must still think of individual interests, and of that greatest of all claims which a human being may make, the claim to assert his individuality, to exercise freely the will and the reason which God has given him. We must emphasize the social interest in the moral and social life of the individual. But we must remember that it is the life of a free-willing being.

V

THE PIONEERS AND THE LAW

IN the highly organized urban life of today we do not always remember how near we are to the pioneer. Less than a century ago the author of the Leatherstocking tales could write of central New York as newly redeemed from the wilderness. The grandfathers of men now living were pioneers in the states formed from the Northwest Territory. The fathers of the present population of the states immediately west of the Mississippi were pioneers there and many of the present generation were brought up under pioneer conditions. Men are still living who were pioneers on the Pacific coast and the beginnings of California are no further back than the span of one life. A great and populous state of the Southwest was opened to settlement by the white man in the last decade of the nineteenth century and has been developed in the present century. The moment one passes beyond the narrow fringe of original settlements along the Atlantic coast, he has but to scratch the surface in order to find the frontier.

"There are features of American democracy," says Professor Sumner, "which are inexplicable unless one understands . . . frontier society. Some of our greatest political abuses have come from transferring to our now large and crowded cities maxims and usages which were convenient and harmless in backwoods country towns." This is no less true of many of our more serious legal abuses. In particular many crudities in judicial organization and procedure are demonstrably legacies of the frontier. Moreover the spirit of American law of the nineteenth century was sensibly affected by the spirit of the pioneer.

For most practical purposes American judicial history begins after the Revolution. Administration of justice in colonial America was at first executive and legislative, and these types of non-judicial justice persisted well into the last century. Again with a few conspicuous exceptions the courts before and for some time after the Revolution were made up largely of untrained magistrates who administered justice according to their common sense and the light of nature with some guidance from legislation. Until the Revolution in most of the colonies it was not considered necessary or even expedient to have judges learned in the law. Of the three justices of the Superior Court in New Hampshire after independence, one was a clergyman and another a physician. A judge of the highest court of Rhode Island from 1814 to 1818 was a blacksmith, and the chief justice of that state from 1819 to 1826 was a farmer. When James Kent went upon the bench in New York in 1791, he could say with entire truth: "There were no reports or state precedents. The opinions from the bench were delivered *ore tenus*. We had no law of our own and nobody knew what [the law] was."

Our judicial organization, then, and the great body of our American common law are the work of the last quarter of the eighteenth century and the first half of the nineteenth century. On the other hand our great cities and the social and legal problems to which they give rise are of the last half of the nineteenth century, and, indeed, the pressing problems do not become acute until the last quarter of that century. Our largest city now contains in three hundred and twenty-six square miles a larger and infinitely more varied population than the whole thirteen states contained when the federal constitution was adopted. But New York City did not attain a population of one million till about 1880; and questions of sanitation and housing were first urged after the Civil War. Such commonwealths as the states west of the Missouri, each of which, with a population not much exceeding a million, occupies an area considerably greater than England and Wales, represent more nearly the conditions for which the American judicial organization was developed and for which the common law of England was made over into a law for America.

To understand the administration of justice in American cities at the end of the nineteenth century, we must perceive the problems of the administration of justice in a homogeneous pioneer or rural community of the first half of the nineteenth century and the difficulties with which lawyers and jurists had to contend in meeting those problems; we must perceive the attitude of such a community toward legal procedure and its conception of the nature and function of a trial; we must perceive its attitude toward government and administration and its rooted objection to supervision and restraint.

In the homogeneous pioneer or rural community of the first half of the nineteenth century, the administration of justice involved three problems: (1) To receive the English common law, or to find somewhere else a basis for legal development, and to work out upon the basis adopted a system of principles and rules adapted to America; (2) to decentralize the administration of justice so as to bring justice to every man's door; and (3) to devise a criminal law and criminal procedure sufficient to deal with the occasional criminal and the criminal of passion in a homogeneous community, of vigorous pioneer race, restrained already for the most part by deep religious conviction and strict moral training.

Chief of these problems was the one first named, the problem of working out a system of rules and principles applicable to America. It has long been the orthodox view that the colonists brought the common law with them and that the English law has obtained in this country from the beginning. But this is only a legal theory. In fact the colonies began with all manner of experiments in administering justice without law and it was not till the middle of the eighteenth century that the setting up of a system of courts and the rise of a custom of studying law in England began to make for a general administration of justice according to English law. Just prior to the Revolution the wide-spread study of Blackstone, whose first edition appeared in 1765, gave great impetus to the reception of the common law. But as late as 1791 the law was so completely at large in New York that the genius of a Kent was needed to make the common law the law of that state.

After the Revolution the public was extremely hostile to England and to all that was English and it was impossible for the common law to escape the odium of its English origin. Judges and legislators were largely influenced by this popular feeling and there was no well-trained bar to resist it. In Philadelphia there were a number of great lawyers, and there were good lawyers here and there throughout the country. But the bulk of the profession was made up of men who had come from the Revolutionary armies or from the halls of the Continental Congress and had brought with them many bitter feelings and often but scanty knowledge of the law. It was natural that they should resent any serious investigation of the English authorities and perhaps endeavor to palliate their lack of information by a show of patriotism. Moreover a large and influential party were enthusiastically attached to France and not only denounced English law because it was English but were inclined to call for a reception of French law. "The citation of English decisions in the opinions of the courts," says Loyd, "greatly exasperated the radical element. What were these precedents but the rags of despotism, who were the judges that rendered them but tyrants, sycophants, oppressors of the people and enemies of liberty." The legal muck-raker of today wields a feeble pen in comparison with his predecessor of the first half of the last century. Under the influence of such ideas, New Jersey, Pennsylvania and Kentucky legislated against citation of English decisions in the courts. There was a rule against such citations in New Hampshire, and more than one judge elsewhere had his fling at the English authorities cited before him.

In part this opposition to the reception of the common law was political. In large part, however, it was but a phase of the opposition of the frontiersman to scientific law. "The unthinking sons of the sagebrush," says Owen Wister, "ill tolerate anything which stands for discipline, good order and obedience; and the man who lets another command him they despise." In this they but represent the feelings of the outposts of civilization everywhere. As numbers increase there is a greater interest in general security. But even then in the rude pioneer community the main point is to keep the peace. Tribunals with power to enforce their judgments are the most pressing need. There the refined, scientific law that weighs and balances and deliberates and admits of argument is out of place. A few simple rules which everyone understands and a swift and decisive tribunal best serve such a community. The customary law of the mining country from 1849 to 1866 largely repeated in this respect the experience of the Atlantic coast down to the Revolution. In the next stage, as wealth increases, commerce develops and society becomes more complex, the social interests in the security of acquisitions and in the security of transactions call imperatively for certainty and uniformity in the administration of justice and hence demand rules. But, as we have seen, at the beginning of the nineteenth century American law was undeveloped and uncertain. Administration of justice by lay judges, by executive officers and by legislatures was crude, unequal, and often partisan, if not corrupt. The prime requirement was rule and system, whereby to guarantee uniformity, equality and certainty. And, since in the nature of things rules may not be laid down in advance for every case, this meant that a scientific development of law was inevitable.

Scientific development of American law was retarded and even warped by the frontier spirit surviving the frontier. The effects of the opposition to an educated well-trained bar and to an independent, experienced, permanent judiciary, which are legacies of the Jefferson Brick era of American politics have been spoken of on a former occasion. It will suffice here to recall the lack of interest in universality and fostering of local peculiarities which are so characteristic of our legal system. In part Puritanism must share the responsibility. But in large part this spirit in American law is a remnant of the frontier repugnance to scientific law and the insistence of the pioneer that his judges decide offhand without study of what other judges may have done in European monarchies or in effete communities to the eastward.

Again, the insistence upon the exact working out of rules and the devotion to that end of the whole machinery of justice, which is so characteristic of nineteenth-century America, is due in great part to pioneer jealousy of governmental action. A pioneer or a sparsely settled rural community is content with and prefers the necessary minimum of government. The social interest in general security requires a certain amount of governmental machinery. It requires civil and criminal tribunals and rules and standards of decision to be applied therein. But when every farm was for the most part sufficient unto itself the chief concern was that the governmental agencies set up to secure this social interest might interfere unduly with individual interests. This pioneer jealousy of governmental action coöperated with the Puritan idea of consociation and the eighteenth-century idea of the rights of man to exalt individual interests and put all possible checks upon organized social control. There must be no magisterial or administrative or judicial discretion. If men had to be governed, it must be by known rules of the law.

Thus the chief problem of the formative period of our American legal system was to discover and lay down rules, to develop a system of certain and detailed rules which on the one hand would meet the requirements of American life, and, on the other hand, would tie down the magistrate by leaving as little to his personal judgment and discretion as possible, would leave as much as possible to the initiative of the individual and would keep down all governmental and official action to the minimum required for the harmonious coexistence of the individual and of the whole. This problem determined the whole course of our legal development until the last quarter of the nineteenth century. Moreover it determined our system of courts and our judicial organization. Above all else we sought to insure an efficient machine for the development of law by judicial decision. For a time this was the chief function of our highest courts. For a time it was meet that John Doe suffer for the commonwealth's sake. Often it was less important to decide the particular cause justly than to work out a sound and just rule for the future. Hence for a century the chief energies of our courts were turned toward the development of our case law and the judicial hierarchy was set up with this purpose in view. It could not be expected that a system of courts constructed chiefly for such purposes would be able to deal effectively with the litigation of an urban community of today in which men look to legislatures to make rules and to courts to dispose of controversies.

A second problem in the formative period of American law was to decentralize the administration of justice so as to bring justice to every man in a sparsely settled community. The system of English courts at the Revolution was too arbitrary and involved to serve as a model to be followed in detail in this country. But overlooking concurrent jurisdiction and some historical anomalies, a general outline might be perceived which was the model of American judicial systems. To begin at the bottom, this was: (1) Local peace magistrates and local inferior courts for petty causes; (2) a central court of general jurisdiction at law and over crimes, with provision for local trial of causes at circuit and review of civil trials in bank in the central court; (3) a central court of equity in which causes were heard in one place, though testimony was taken in the locality; (4) a separate court with probate jurisdiction; and (5) a supreme court of review. In the United States all but five or six jurisdictions merged the second and third. But with that salutary act of unification most of our jurisdictions stopped. Indeed for a season there was no need for unification. The defects in the foregoing scheme that appealed to the formative period of American judicial organization lay in the second and third of the tribunals above described, namely the central court of law and the central court of equity. In a country of long distances in a period of slow communication and expensive travel, these central courts entailed intolerable hardship upon litigants. It was a prime necessity to bring justice to every man's back door. Accordingly in most states we set up a number of local courts of general jurisdiction at law and in equity and our policy has been one of multiplication of courts ever since. Nowhere is radical change so much needed as in the organization of our courts. In almost all of our states the whole plan of judicial organization, adapted to a pioneer, rural, agricultural community of the first half of the nineteenth century, is in the way of efficient disposition of the litigation of the industrial and urban community of today.

A hundred years ago the problem seemed to be how to hold down the administration of punitive justice and protect the individual from oppression under the guise thereof rather than how to make the criminal law an effective agency for securing social interests. English criminal law had been developed by judicial experience to meet violent crimes in an age of force and violence. Later the necessities of more civilized times had led to the development in the court of Star Chamber of what is now the common law as to misdemeanors. Thus one part of the English law of crimes, as our fathers found it, was harsh and brutal, as befitted a law made to put down murder by violence, robbery, rape and cattle stealing in a rough and ready community. Another part seemed to involve dangerous magisterial discretion, as might have been expected of a body of law made in the council of Tudor and Stuart kings in an age of extreme theories of royal prerogative. The colonists had had experience of the close connection of criminal law with politics. The pioneers who had preserved the memory of this experience were not concerned solely to do away with the brutality of the old law as to felonies. Even more their constant fear of political oppression through the criminal law led them and the generation following, which had imbibed their ideas, to exaggerate the complicated, expensive and dilatory machinery of a common-law prosecution, lest some safeguard of individual liberty be overlooked, to give excessive power to juries and to limit or even cut off the power of the trial judge to control the trial and hold the jury to its province. Nor did these enfeeblings of punitive justice work much evil in a time and in places where crime, except possibly the feud and the duel, on which the community looked indulgently, was rare and abnormal, where, therefore, the community did not require the swift-moving punitive justice, adjusted to the task of enforcing a voluminous criminal code against a multitude of offenders, which we demand today.

In Fennimore Cooper's Pioneers, the story opens with a striking picture of central New York in 1833, a region which, as we are told, had been a wilderness forty years before. Above all the author attributes its prosperity to mild laws and to the spirit of the pioneer. "The whole district," he says, "is hourly exhibiting how much can be done, in even a rugged country, and with a severe climate, under the dominion of mild laws, and where every man feels a direct interest in the prosperity of a commonwealth of which he knows himself a part." This is the spirit of our American common-law polity. It presupposes a homogeneous population which is jealous of its rights and in sympathy with the institutions of government. It presupposes a public which is intrinsically law abiding, even if inclined under provocation to vindicate public justice by rough and ready methods. It presupposes a people which for the most part will conform to rules of law when they are ascertained and made known, so that the chief concern of courts and of the state is to settle what is the law. It presupposes a public which in the jury box may be relied upon to enforce law and vindicate justice between man and man intelligently and steadfastly. In other words, our common-law polity presupposes an American farming community of the first half of the nineteenth century; a situation as far apart as the poles from what our legal system has had to meet in the endeavor to administer justice to great urban communities at the end of the nineteenth and in the twentieth century.

American procedure, as it had developed through judicial decision, professional usage and legislation in the last century, shows the hand of the pioneer even more plainly. It requires no great study of our procedure to enable us to perceive that many of its features, taking the country as a whole, were determined by the conditions of rural communities of seventy-five or one hundred years ago. Many of its features are more appropriate to rural, agricultural communities, where in intervals of work, the farmer, remote from the distractions of city life, found his theater in the court house and looked to politics and litigation for amusement, than to modern urban communities. For instance, if I have read American judicial biography aright, no small part of the exaggerated importance of the advocate in an American court of justice, of the free rein, one might almost say the license, afforded him, while the judge must sit by and administer the rules of the combat, may be traced to frontier conditions and frontier modes of thought. When the farmers of the county have gathered to hear a forensic display they resent the direction of a verdict on a point of law which cuts off the anticipated flow of eloquence. They resent judicial limitation of the time for argument, since the audience is to be considered as well as the court and the litigants. Hence legislation tying down the trial judge in the interests of untrammeled advocacy has its origin on the frontier. In particular it may be shown that legislation restricting the charge of the court has grown out of the desire of eloquent counsel, of a type so dear to the pioneer community, to deprive not merely the trial judge but the law of all influence upon trials and to leave everything to be disposed of on the arguments. Moreover the frontier spectator in the forensic arena is not unlike his urban brother who looks on at a game of baseball. He soon learns the points of the game and knows and appreciates those who can play it.

In a book of reminiscences of an eminent lawyer there is a chapter entitled "Country Practice of the Law" which describes the writer's experience in the western part of Massachusetts in 1861. He tells of a case where, in a prosecution for malicious injury to real estate, the case was that a wooden pump had been taken out of a well in mere wanton mischief. Counsel contended that there was no malicious injury to real estate since the land was not injured and the pump itself was personalty so that the complaint should have been for malicious injury to personal property. To show this he argued that if a pump were realty there would have to be a conveyance by deed of sale every time one was sold. The magistrate was duly impressed and discharged the accused, but, being a conscientious man, proceeded to draw up a new complaint for malicious injury to personal property, upon which the accused were re-arrested and put upon trial. Thereupon the same counsel cited authorities, which were unanimous and conclusive, that the pump in the well and annexed thereto for permanent use was a fixture and so not personal property. The justice could not deny the force of these decisions and was obliged to discharge the accused upon this charge also, so that they escaped. But, we are told, "the magistrate enjoyed the joke upon himself as much as the rest of us. In fact," the author continues, "many of these legal trials at the time were looked upon as huge jokes." Elsewhere he says: "The whole contest was looked upon as a contest of wits, and if a person prevailed on account of knowing more than the other party, it was not considered at all derogatory to his character that he should use that knowledge in any way that was best suited to the interest of his client." The ethics of such a contest were the ethics of the professional baseball game. I need not say that we have got well beyond this in professional ethics today. But our procedure is still too much in the spirit of which such advocacy is only an extreme manifestation.

The pioneer has influenced American judicial procedure in another way. On the frontier "everyone that was in distress and everyone that was in debt and everyone that was discontented gathered themselves" to begin life anew. Hence the attitude of the pioneer was not favorable to the creditor seeking to enforce his claim and the legislation of our pioneer jurisdictions was often what might have been expected of the cave of Adullam. Extravagant powers in juries, curtailment of the powers of trial judges, an abattis of procedural obstacles in the way of plaintiffs and a vested right in errors of procedure on the part of defendants—all these institutions of American procedure grow out of the desire of the frontier community to shield those who had fled thereto from the exactions of their creditors. Later, when these communities had borrowed heavily from their older neighbors in developing their natural resources there was a strong local interest in preserving these institutions. The very spirit of procedure in some parts of the United States is so tinctured by frontier favor to debtors that improvements in the direction of increased effectiveness in the judicial machinery can come but slowly. All this is quite alien to common-law modes of thought. But it has affected common-law procedure in America not a little.

What Dean Wigmore has called the sporting theory of justice, the idea that judicial administration of justice is a game to be played to the bitter end, no doubt has its roots in Anglo-American character and is closely connected with the individualism of the common law. Yet it was fostered by the frontier attitude toward litigation and it has flourished chiefly in recent times in tribunals such as the Texas Court of Criminal Appeals, where the memory of the frontier is still green. Moreover the rise of a class of habitual defendants, who are compelled to fall back upon procedural niceties through the unwillingness of juries to judge them according to law or even to do them justice, and the rise of a class of habitual plaintiffs' lawyers, who rely on sympathy and prejudice rather than law, and resent judicial interference to enforce law or preserve justice, have served to keep the spirit of frontier procedure alive in a wholly different environment. Technical procedure is neither a necessary check on the magistrate in the interest of liberty nor a device to advance justice. It is a remnant of the mechanical modes of trial in the beginnings of our law, developed in the eighteenth century in an age of formal over-refinement, fostered and even further developed in the pioneer or rural American communities of the last century, and turned to new uses in the standing warfare between professional plaintiffs' lawyers and habitual defendants produced more recently by the conditions of tort litigation in industrial and urban communities.

Reference has been made in other connections to the nineteenth-century aggravation of the common-law attitude toward administration. The political ideas of the seventeenth century growing out of the contests between the courts and the crown, Puritanism, and the political ideas of the eighteenth century all contributed to this attitude. But the exaggeration of it in the last century was in no small degree the result of the pioneer's jealousy of government and administration and his rooted objection to supervision and restraint. So also the jealousy of social legislation that developed in the last quarter of the nineteenth century, the insistence upon liberty of contract and the right to pursue a lawful calling as guaranteed to the individual and beyond the reach of legislation, result in part from the feeling on the part of the pioneer that he should be let alone and that he was ruled best when he was ruled least. In both these instances, Puritan and pioneer, working with materials fashioned in the contests between courts and crown in the seventeenth century, were able to put checks upon the enactment and enforcement of social legislation in this country for forty years after English lawmaking had definitely changed front.

How great a strain is put upon our legal and judicial institutions by the stamp of the pioneer, which they acquired in the formative period, may be seen by taking up the chief problems of administration of justice in the American city of today and perceiving how little our institutions are adjusted to them.

Demand for socialization of law, in the United States, has come almost wholly, if not entirely from the city. We have no class of agricultural laborers demanding protection. The call to protect men from themselves, to regulate housing, to enforce sanitation, to inspect the supply of milk, to prevent imposition upon ignorant and credulous immigrants, to protect the small investor of savings from get-rich-quick enterprises, to regulate conditions of labor and provide a minimum wage, and the conditions that require us to heed this call, have come from the cities. But our legal system has had to meet this demand upon the basis of rules and principles developed for rural communities or small towns—for men who needed no protection other than against aggression and overreaching between equals dealing in matters which each understood. Less than a generation ago we were echoing the outcry of our fathers against governmental paternalism. Today, not only have we swung over to this condition in large measure, as our increasing apparatus of commissions and boards and inspectors testifies every day, but we are beginning to call for what has been styled governmental maternalism to meet the conditions of our great urban communities. Although much has been done and comparatively rapid progress is now making, it is perhaps still a chief problem to work out a system of legal administration of justice which will secure the social interest in the moral and social life of every individual under the circumstances of the modern city, upon the basis of rules and principles devised primarily to protect the interest in general security in a rural community of seventy-five years ago.

Again, the demand for organization of justice and improvement of legal procedure comes from our cities. It is a significant circumstance that in the debates upon this subject in the past fifteen years in our bar associations, national and state, the city lawyer has asserted that reform was imperative, while the country lawyer has contended that the evils were greatly exaggerated and that grave changes were wholly unnecessary; the city lawyer has been urging ambitious programs of reform and the country lawyer has been defeating them. A modern judicial organization and a modern procedure would, indeed, be a real service to country as well as to city. But the pressure comes from the city, to which we are vainly endeavoring to adjust the old machinery. Courts in our great cities as they are now organized are subjected to almost overwhelming pressure by an accumulated mass of litigation. Usually they sit almost the year round, and yet they tire out parties and witnesses with long delays, and in some jurisdictions dispose of much of their business so hastily and imperfectly that reversals and retrials are continually required. Such a condition may be found in the courts of general jurisdiction in nearly all of our cities. To deal adequately with the civil litigation of a city, to enforce the mass of police regulations required by conditions of urban life, and to make the criminal law effective to secure social interests, we must obviate waste of judicial power, save time and conserve effort. There was no need of this when our judicial system was framed. There is often little need of it in the country today. In the city the waste of time and money in doing things that are wholly unnecessary results in denial of justice.

A third problem of the administration of justice in the modern city is to make adequate provision for petty litigation, to provide for disposing quickly, inexpensively and justly of the litigation of the poor, for the collection of debts in a shifting population, and for the great volume of small controversies which a busy, crowded population, diversified in race and language necessarily engenders. It is here that the administration of justice touches immediately the greatest number of people. It is here that the great mass of an urban population, whose experience of law in the past has been too often experience only of the arbitrary discretion of police officers, might be made to feel that the law is a living force for securing their individual as well as their collective interests. For there is a strong social interest in the moral and social life of the individual. If the will of the individual is subjected arbitrarily to the will of others because the means of protection are too cumbersome and expensive to be available for one of his means against an aggressive opponent who has the means or the inclination to resist, there is an injury to society at large. The most real grievance of the mass of the people against American law has not been with respect to the rules of substantive law but rather with respect to the enforcing machinery which too often makes the best of rules nugatory in action. Municipal courts in some of our larger cities are beginning to relieve this situation. But taking the country as a whole, it is so obvious that we have almost ceased to remark it, that in petty causes, that is with respect to the everyday rights and wrongs of the great majority of an urban community, the machinery whereby rights are secured practically defeats rights by making it impracticable to assert them when they are infringed.

Many causes have contributed to this neglect of provision for petty litigation which has disgraced American justice. Two of them at least are attributable to the conditions of pioneer justice. One has been noticed in another connection, namely that we have had to work out a body of substantive law for large causes and small alike in an age of rapid growth and rapid change. Hence we have studied the making of law sedulously. For more than a century in this country we have been engaged in developing in judicial experience a body of principles and a body of rules as deductions therefrom to accord as nearly as may be with the requirements of justice. This is true especially of that most important part of our law which is to be found in the reports of adjudicated cases. Almost the whole energy of our judicial system has been employed in working out a consistent, logical, minutely precise body of precedents. But while our eyes have been fixed upon the abstract rules, which are but the means of achieving justice, the results which we obtain every day in actual causes have escaped our attention. If the dilatory machinery of enforcement succeeds finally in applying the principle to the cause, we may be assured that in the very great majority of causes the result will be what it should be. But our failure to devote equal attention to application and enforcement of law has too often allowed the machinery designed to give effect to legal rules to defeat the end of law in its actual operation. The other cause referred to is that our procedure, as has been seen, was determined largely by the conditions of rural communities of seventy-five or one hundred years ago. Hence when better provision for petty causes is urged, many repeat the stock saying that litigation ought to be discouraged. It will not do to say to the population of modern cities that the practical cutting off of all petty litigation, by which theoretically the rights of the average man are to be maintained, is a good thing because litigation ought to be discouraged. Litigation for the sake of litigation ought to be discouraged. But this is the only form of petty litigation which survives the discouragements involved in American judicial organization and procedure. In truth, the idea that litigation is to be discouraged, proper enough, in so far as it refers to amicable adjustment of what ought to be so adjusted, has its roots chiefly in the obvious futility of litigation under the conditions of procedure which have obtained in the immediate past. It is much more appropriate to frontier and rural communities where a lawsuit was a game and a trial a spectacle than to modern urban communities. Moreover, there is danger that in discouraging litigation we encourage wrongdoing, and it requires very little experience in the legal aid societies in any of our cities to teach us that we have been doing that very thing. Of all peoples in the world, we ought to have been the most solicitous for the rights of the poor, no matter how petty the causes in which they are to be vindicated. Unhappily, except as the organization of municipal courts in recent years has been bringing about a change, we have been callous to the just claims of this class of controversies.

Application and enforcement of law are regarded as the central questions in modern legal science. These questions are especially acute in the United States because our polity has committed so much to courts that elsewhere is left to the executive and legislative departments. They are especially acute in American cities because in these cities the demands made of the courts increase continually. In these communities the Puritan conception of law as a guide to the conscience and the pioneer conception that the courts exist chiefly to work out rules for a new country are wholly inadequate. The pioneer conception of enforcement through individual initiative is even more inadequate. Both the law and the agencies that administer the law, shaped by such conceptions, are unequal to the burden put upon them by the circumstances of city life and the modern feeling that law is a product of conscious and determinate human will. This is the more apparent in application and enforcement of law in a heterogeneous community. Under the influence of the theory of natural rights and of the actual equality in pioneer society, American common law assumed that there were no classes and that normally men dealt with one another on equal terms and at arm's length; so that courts at the end of the nineteenth century were loth to admit, if they would admit at all, the validity of legislation which recognized the classes that do in fact exist in our industrial society and the inequality in point of fact that may exist in bargainings between them. It assumed also that every normal part of the community was zealous to maintain its rights and would take the initiative in doing so. Not a little friction has resulted from application of rules based upon this theoretical equality in communities divided into classes with divergent interests. A great deal of ineffectiveness has come from application of common-law principles, developed to an extreme in adapting them to pioneer communities, to elements of the city population which do not understand our individualism and our tenderness of individual liberty, and from reliance upon individual initiative in case of other elements which by instinct and training are suspicious of authority and of magistrates. Mr. Train's book, Crime, Criminals and the Camorra, shows vividly how fear of courts, bred of conditions in another land, may lead immigrants to tolerate gross oppression rather than to go to the law for relief.

Finally the social workers in our cities have had to wrestle with the problem of freeing administration from the rigid limitations imposed in the last century. The attempt to confine administrative action within the narrowest possible limits gave us at the end of the nineteenth century a multitude of rules which hindered, as against few which helped. Regulation of public utilities, factory inspection, food inspection, tenement house inspection and building laws have compelled us to turn more and more from the criminal law to the administrative supervision and prevention which the pioneer abhorred. So thoroughly did he hamper administration that the reaction has given rise to a real danger that we go too far in the opposite direction and withdraw such matters wholly from the domain of law. The pioneer's public and administrative law cannot endure. We must work over the whole along new lines.

Reviewing the influence of the pioneer upon our law, it may be conceded that we owe not a little to the vigorous good sense of the judges who made over the common law of England for our pioneer communities. Science might have sunk into pedantry where strong sense gave to America a practical system in which the traditional principles were made to work in a new environment. On the other hand this rapid development of law in a pioneer environment left a bad mark on our administration of justice. The descendants of the frontiersman have been slow to learn that democracy is not necessarily a synonym of vulgarity and provincialism; that the court of a sovereign people may be surrounded by dignity which is the dignity of that people; that order and decorum conduce to the dispatch of judicial business, while disorder and easy-going familiarity retard it; that a counsellor at law may be a gentleman with fine professional feelings without being a member of a privileged caste; that a trial may be an agency of justice among a free people without being a forensic gladiatorial show; that a judge may be an independent, experienced, expert specialist without being a tyrant. In the federal courts and in an increasing number of the states something has been done to secure the dignity of judicial tribunals. But the country over there is still much to do. Not the least factor in making courts and bar efficient agencies for justice will be restoration of common-law ideals and deliverance of both from the yoke of crudity and coarseness which the frontier sought to impose on them.

VI

THE PHILOSOPHY OF LAW IN THE NINETEENTH CENTURY

IN primitive society an injured person may obtain redress by self-help, by the help of the gods or of their ministers, or in a limited class of cases and on compliance with certain procedural forms, by the help of the political organization. In antiquity, when the bond of kinship was the strongest bond in society, the first meant redress by the help of oneself and of his kinsmen, so that the staple institutions of primitive society are reprisals, private war and the blood feud. But these institutions are inimical to the social interest in general security and so more and more appeals for redress are made to the state. Self-help and private war are regulated and repressed until the latter is wholly put down and the former becomes exceptional. Thus in its beginnings law is a means toward the peaceable ordering of society. It stands beside religion and morality as one of the regulative agencies by which men are restrained and the social interest in general security is protected. Moreover this character of a regulative agency, of a means toward a peaceable ordering of the community, is retained to the end, although other purposes are added as it develops. In this first stage of legal evolution men acquire the conception of a peaceable ordering of society through the peaceable adjustment of controversies.

A second stage of legal evolution has been referred to in a former lecture under the name of "the strict law." In this stage, law has definitely prevailed as the regulative agency of society and the state has prevailed as the organ of social control. Self-help and self-redress have been definitely superseded for all but exceptional causes. Normally men appeal only to the state to redress wrongs. Hence the body of rules determining the cases in which men may appeal to the state for help comes to define indirectly the substance of rights and thus indirectly to point out and limit the interests recognized and secured. When this point has been reached, two causes operate to produce a rigid system, namely, fear of arbitrary exercise of the power of state assistance to individual victims of wrong, and survival of ideas from primitive law when deliberate deviation from sacred texts and settled customs was held impious and dangerous. Accordingly the chief end sought is certainty. The cases in which the state will interfere, the mode in which it will interfere and the manner in which its interference may be invoked are defined in an utterly hard and fast way. The rules of law are wholly inelastic and inflexible. Also the law is highly formal. It refuses to look beyond and behind the form, for forms admit of no debate. At any rate one may know whether the appointed form has been pursued. Thus the strict law is indifferent to the moral aspects of conduct or of transactions that satisfy its letter and so further development becomes imperative. But the strict law gives us as permanent contributions the ideas of certainty and uniformity and of rule and form as means thereto.

A stage of liberalization, which may be called the stage of equity or natural law, succeeds the strict law. This stage is represented in Roman law by the classical period (the empire to Diocletian), in English law by the rise of the Court of Chancery and development of equity, in the law of Continental Europe by the period of the law-of-nature school, that is, the seventeenth and eighteenth centuries. The watchword of the stage of strict law was certainty. The watchword of this stage is morality or some phrase of ethical import such as equity and good conscience. The former stage insists on uniformity, the latter on morality; the former on form, the latter on justice in the ethical sense; the former on remedies, the latter on duties; the former on rule, the latter on reason. The capital ideas of the stage of equity or natural law are the identification of law with morals, the conception of duty and attempt to make moral duties into legal duties, and reliance upon reason rather than upon arbitrary rule to keep down caprice and eliminate the personal element in the administration of justice. Aside from liberalization of the law, the permanent contributions of this stage of legal evolution are the conception of good faith and moral conduct, to be attained through reason, ethical solution of controversies and enforcement of duties. But the endeavor to make law and morals coincide and to reach an ethical solution of each particular controversy gives too wide a scope to judicial discretion so that at first the administration of justice in this stage is too personal and too uncertain. This excess of margin for discretion is corrected by a gradual fixing of rules and consequent stiffening of the legal system. Moral principles, having acquired the character of legal rules, are carried out to logical consequences until the original principle is lost among the derived rules, or are developed as mere abstractions and thus are deprived of their purely moral character. In this way transition takes place to the next stage, which may be called the maturity of law.

As a result of the stiffening process by which the undue fluidity of law and over-wide scope for discretion involved in the identification of law and morals are gradually corrected, there comes to be a body of law with the stable and certain qualities of the strict law yet liberalized by the conceptions devolped by equity or natural law. In this stage of matured legal system, the watchwords are equality and security. It derives the idea of equality partly from the insistence of the strict law that the same remedy shall always be applied to the same formal situation and partly from the insistence of equity or natural law on treating all human beings as legal persons and upon recognizing full legal capacity in all persons possessed of normal mind and years of discretion. Hence its idea of equality has two elements; equality of operation of legal rules and equality of opportunity to exercise one's will and employ one's substance. It derives its idea of security from the strict law, but finds it modified by the ideas of the stage of equity or natural law that legal results should flow from will rather than from form and that one person should not be enriched unjustly at the expense of another because of form and without intention. In consequence, its idea of security includes two elements: everyone is to be secured in his interests against aggression by others and others are to be permitted to acquire from him or to exact from him only through his will that they do so or through his breach of rules devised to secure others in like interests.

To insure equality, the maturity of law again insists strongly upon certainty and in this respect is comparable in many ways to the stage of the strict law. To insure security it insists upon property and contract as fundamental ideas. Our bills of rights bring this out in their guarantees of life, liberty and property.

Liberty in such connections was taken to mean in the nineteenth century, and is still sometimes taken to mean, that the individual shall not be held legally unless for a fault, unless for an act on his part which infringes another's right, and that another shall not be permitted to exact of him except as and to the extent he has willed a relation to which the law in advance attached such power to exact. The same idea appears in the modern Roman law in the insistence upon will as the central point in legal transactions and the nineteenth-century attempt to make the Anglo-American law of contracts conform to the Roman conception was quite in accord with the spirit of the time.

Along with liberty the maturity of law puts property, that is, the security of acquisitions. But one of these acquisitions may be a power to exact from a promisor. Accordingly contract acquires a property aspect. The law is regarded as existing to secure the power of contracting freely and the right to exact a performance freely promised as widely as possible. Moreover in this stage even personality acquires a property aspect. The power of the individual to make contracts freely is thought of primarily as a sort of asset. In other words, physical integrity and free motion and locomotion, physical and mental, are thought of as species of natural acquisitions, as it were, so that the security of acquisitions, which is conceived to be the main end of the law, includes (1) natural acquisitions, that is, what nature has given one in the way of physical and mental powers, (2) what one has acquired through the position in which he found himself in society, and (3) what one has acquired through the free exercise of his natural powers. In the maturity of law men may be willing to agree that acquisitions of the second type shall be restricted greatly or even cut off for the future, but all idea of interfering with what has been so acquired in the past appears intolerable. From the point of view of this stage of legal development, Mr. Choate was entirely justified when he said, in his argument in the Income Tax Cases, that a fundamental object of the law was "preservation of the rights of private property."

If, as I believe, the law has entered definitely upon a new stage, in many ways analogous to the stage of equity or natural law, as the maturity of law was analogous to the strict law, one may venture to pronounce as to the permanent contribution to the science of administering justice made by the period from which we are passing. Obviously its important legal institutions are property and contract. Its contribution seems to be the thorough working out of individual rights. Accordingly the philosophy of law in the nineteenth century put individual rights at the foundation of the legal system.

At the end of the eighteenth century transition from the stage of equity or natural law to the stage of maturity of law was complete. On the Continent, codification had begun with the draft code of Frederick the Great in 1749 and in 1804 the French civil code summed up the work of the eighteenth-century jurists and furnished the model for practically all the codes of the Roman-law world until the Germans set a new model in 1896. In the common-law world Lord Mansfield had incorporated the law merchant in English law, equity had crystallized so that in 1818 Lord Eldon could say that the principles of equity were almost as fixed and uniform as the rules of the common law and bills of rights in America were codifying the natural rights of man. The completion of this rigidifying process, which had been going on for more than a century, coincided with an epoch-making change in the philosophy of law. The theory of natural law had done its work of liberalization and modernization and had become for the time an agency of stabilization. Men thought it possible to discover a body of fixed and immutable principles, from which a complete system, perfect in every detail, might be deduced by purely logical operations, and held it the duty of the jurist to find them and of the legislator to promulgate the deductions in the form of a code. The principles also, they conceived, were to be discovered once for all by reason since they were mere expressions of abstract human nature; they were the principles of reason inherent in the conduct of the abstract individual. But the possibilities of this juristic method had been exhausted. The rationalizing legal philosophy of Grotius had accomplished its task. It was no longer capable of making for growth in the law, and for a season growth was not needed. The demand of the time was not for growth but for system and classification and analysis in order to produce certainty and insure security. Philosophy was asked to make law stable as two centuries before men had turned to it to make law fluid. Although eighteenth-century natural law had led to codification and had become an absolute system it was not equal to the philosophical problem of nineteenth-century law. It left too much to the individual judgment and conscience to afford a satisfactory theoretical foundation. Indeed, the philosophical anarchist builds on the doctrine of natural rights and on the natural-law conception of the individual conscience as the ultimate arbiter as to duties of obedience. The time was ripe, therefore, when the received theory of natural law got its death-blow at the hands of Immanuel Kant. He undermined the seventeenth- and eighteenth-century foundations of philosophical jurisprudence and replaced them with a new order of ideas. These new ideas, however, were to serve for the basis of the stable law of the nineteenth century. Hence the present generation, wrestling with legal institutions and legal doctrines fashioned in other eras, often finds them intrenched, however remote their origin, in nineteenth-century philosophy of law.

To Kant and those who followed him more immediately the first problem in law was the relation of law to liberty. He lived in an age of codification, an age of absolute governments, in which there was and it was taken that there had to be external constraint and coercion. But he lived also in the age of the French Revolution, a democratic age in which some other basis than mere authority was required to sustain the arbitrary and authoritative; the age of the classical economics, in which the individual demanded the widest possible freedom of action. Hence the problem was how to reconcile these two ideas—external constraint and individual freedom of action. This question furnishes the clue to all philosophical discussion of the basis of law in the last century. Kant met it by formulating what has come to be known by the significant name of legal justice; by working out the idea of an equal chance to all, exactly as they are, with no artificial or extrinsic handicaps. In other words, he put a new philosophical foundation under the idea of justice as the maximum of individual self-assertion—the idea which came in with the Reformation—and so enabled it to reach its final logical development in the law of the nineteenth century.

Down to Kant, all jurists had been in agreement as to the method of legal science. Much as they might differ as to details, they were agreed in using philosophical method and in postulating a natural law by which all questions were to be tried. As the effect of Kant's demolition of the old natural law came to be felt, for a time philosophical jurisprudence was pushed to the wall, and it is only in the present century that philosophy has begun to regain the place it once held in legal science. The historical and the analytical methods are the methods of nineteenth-century jurisprudence. This is true especially in Anglo-American juristic thought. English and Americans a generation ago were confident that they had effected a complete separation of jurisprudence from philosophy. To a certain extent, it is true, such a separation took place everywhere and we but carried it to an extreme. The need of stability and certainty in the maturity of law and the importance of the social interests in security of acquisitions and security of transactions in a commercial and industrial society called for analytical rather than philosophical method; the task of the jurist was to perfect what he found in the legal system rather than to build anew. Naturally this general tendency of the last century became most pronounced in America since, as has been shown in another connection, American law is a product of the nineteenth century. Our classical period, from the Revolution to the Civil War, is not so much a period of growth as one of adaptation; it was not a creative period, but instead was a period in which received materials were worked over into better form and were developed into a consistent legal system. Hence with all its appearance of growth, it was a period of stability, and in common with the maturity of law everywhere is comparable to the stage of strict law. For in each stage the law is taken to be self-sufficient. Such periods of legal development require and rely upon analysis rather than philosophy. It is in periods of growth, periods in which the law is fluid, periods in which an infusion of ideas from without is making over the law, that philosophy has played a leading rôle in legal history. Hence, on the one hand, philosophy of law is reviving today, as we enter upon the new stage of legal development which has been called the socialization of law, and hence, on the other hand, American law, the product of the nineteenth century, has affected to have no use for philosophy. In practical effect, the result has been to intrench in our legal thinking the absolute ideas which we inherited from the eighteenth century. The naïve natural law of the practitioner, who takes the principles in which he has been trained and with which he is familiar for fundamenta of all law everywhere, the theories of natural law and natural rights which came into our elementary books and our books on constitutional law from Continental publicists of the seventeenth and eighteenth century had their own way with the profession; and later historical jurisprudence which developed a natural law of its own and reached results quite as absolute had its own way in the schools.

Our absolute ideas which have prevailed so largely in American legal thinking come from Grotius in two ways. On the one hand they come through Blackstone, whose preliminary discussions are founded upon Grotius, and on the other hand they come through American publicists in the eighteenth century and the first part of the nineteenth century who followed the Dutch and French publicists and civilians. Chiefly, however, they come from Blackstone. It was only in the present generation that legal education in the majority of our best schools was divorced from Blackstone, and bar examinations in many states still call for a knowledge of this obsolete legal science. Such was the result in practice of our contempt of philosophy of law.

Two movements are represented in eighteenth-century juristic thought. First there is a purely juristic movement, proceeding upon the conception that law is reason, in which the ideas of right and justice are made paramount. In this movement, as we have seen elsewhere, individual rights and justice as the realization of individual rights were put above state and society as permanent absolute realities which state and society existed only to protect. Second, there is a legislative movement in which rights are thought of as the product of the human will, as the outgrowth of a social contract, so that there would be no rights without the social organization and no justice or law but for the political organization; a movement in which law is thought of as emanating from the sovereign and the idea of command of the state or of the general will becomes paramount. Both theories are stated by Blackstone without a hint of their inconsistency. In the nineteenth century, however, they came to divide the field. The second theory passed into political thinking and the science of legislation. Thence, following Bentham, it was taken up by the analytical jurists, who have been dominant in English legal thought since the middle of the last century. But this side of analytical jurisprudence was never congenial in America. The first theory passed into metaphysical and historical jurisprudence. Already accepted by the American lawyer while analytical jurisprudence was formative in England, it came back to him presently in scientific garb from Germany and became a settled conviction.

Five types of philosophy of law in the nineteenth century are of significance for our present purpose. We may call those who adhered to them the metaphysical school, the historical school, the utilitarians, the positivists and the mechanical sociologists. It is a striking example of the way in which the same conclusion may sustain the most divergent philosophical premises that all of these arrived ultimately at the same juristic position by wholly diverse routes and from the most diverse starting points, so that the futility of conscious effort to improve the condition of humanity through the law and the conception of justice as the securing of the maximum of self-assertion became axioms of juristic thought.

While to the eighteenth century justice meant the securing of absolute, eternal, universal natural rights of individuals, Kant held that it meant securing freedom of will to everyone so far as consistent with all other wills. The metaphysical jurists developed this idea. Their fundamental position was that the whole legal system could be deduced from the conception of right and in this way a critique of institutions and doctrines, a sort of ideal system, could be set up. As a rule they carried out Kant's idea of securing the free will into its practical consequence of liberty; of general freedom of action for individuals. Hence in their view the end of law was to secure the widest possible liberty to each individual. The test of right and justice with respect to any institution or doctrine was the amount of abstract individual liberty which it secured. The metaphysical method gradually fell into discredit abroad after the middle of the nineteenth century, although it had representatives in juristic writing to the very end of that century. But through its effect upon the historical school, which controlled legal thought for almost a hundred years, its intensely individualist conception of justice governed in jurisprudence until the rise of the social-philosophical school set jurists to thinking in a new way. Anglo-American jurists paid little or no attention to the systems of the metaphysical school. Its central idea of liberty, however, fitted the eighteenth-century individualism of our law so well that the method of deduction from that idea was gradually adopting when a new and more attractive mode of getting to the same result was furnished by the positivists.

Savigny, the founder of the historical school,

turned Kant's formula of right into one of law. Kant thought of right as a condition in which the will of one was reconciled with the will of another according to a universal rule. Savigny thought of law as the body of rules which determine the bounds within which the activities of each individual are secured a free opportunity. If we adopt an idealistic interpretation of legal history and conceive of the development of law as a gradual unfolding of Kant's idea of right in human experience of administering justice, we shall understand the position of the historical school. For Savigny carried forward one of the two ideas which had been contending in jurisprudence in the eighteenth century. The element in law which the medieval jurists had rested on theology, the seventeenth-century jurists had derived from reason, and the law-of-nature school in the eighteenth century had deduced from the nature of man, Savigny sought to discover through history. In effect the historical school and the metaphysical school were closely akin. Each postulated an ideal law. One sought to discover this ideal law through history, the other sought to find it through logical development of an abstract idea. Indeed, it was not hard to reconcile these views. As the historical jurists adopted the idealistic interpretation of legal history it was possible to say that jurisprudence had two sides. On the one hand it had to do with the historical unfolding of the idea of liberty as men discovered the rules by which to realize it. This was historical jurisprudence. On the other hand, it had to do with the logical unfolding of the principles involved in the abstract conception. This was philosophical jurisprudence. Most of the German expositions of jurisprudence in the latter half of the nineteenth century proceed in this way. Philosopher and historian were agreed that law was found not made. One found it by deduction from a metaphysical principle, the other found it by historical study. Each, one need not say, found an ideal development of the principles of the existing law; the historian because he so interpreted history, the philosopher because he was seldom a lawyer and got his facts and illustrations from the historian.

The doctrines of the German historical school appear to have been taught first in this country in a course of lectures given by Luther S. Cushing at the Harvard Law School in 1849 and published in 1854. It is interesting to note that the late James C. Carter was a law student at Harvard the last year that this course was given; for unless the effect of early training is borne in mind, it is hard to understand how a jurist of his caliber could dogmatically assent to Savigny's views in 1905. But the influence of the historical school did not become marked in America till after 1870, when American students had begun to go to Germany in increasing numbers and German ideas had taken root in our universities. In the meantime another influence had profoundly affected American legal thought. That influence, namely, the political interpretation of legal history and political theory of jurisprudence expounded by Sir Henry Maine, moved in the same direction. I have spoken sufficiently of Maine's political interpretation in other connections. It is enough to say here that his theory of the progress from *status* to contract was so thoroughly adapted to the individualism which characterized the traditional element of our law for other reasons and accorded so well with the absolute ideas which our law books had inherited from the century before, that it soon got complete possession of the field.

As I have said, the historical jurist and the philosophical jurist agreed that law was found, not made, differing only with respect to what it was that was found. The philosophical jurist thought that a principle of justice and right was found and expressed in a rule. The historical jurist conceived that a principle of human action or of social action was found by human experience and was gradually developed into and expressed in a rule. Hence the historical school denied that law was a product of conscious or determinate human will. They doubted the efficacy of legislation, in that it sought to achieve the impossible and to make what cannot be made. They held that the living organs of law were doctrinal writing and judicial decision, whereby the life of a people, expressed in the first instance in its traditional rules of law made itself felt in a gradual development by molding those rules to the conditions of the present.

I would not be understood as denying or forgetting that this historical school did many great things for the science of law. But its exclusive reign in American juristic thought in the past fifty years brought out its worst side. For the historical school also worked *a priori* and gave us theories fully as absolute as those of the school of natural law. Each deduced from and tested existing doctrines by a fixed, arbitrary, unchangeable standard. When the historical jurists overthrew the premises of the philosophical school of the preceding century they preserved the method of their predecessors, merely substituting new premises. They were sure that universal principles of jurisprudence were not to be found by deduction from the nature of the abstract individual. But they did not doubt that there were such principles and they expected to find them through historical investigation. In the United States we carried this further than elsewhere, since the merger of the common-law rights of Englishmen in the rights of man seemed to show that here at least universal principles had been worked out in the course of legal history. Even now, on the whole, the basis of all deduction is the classical common law. No system of natural law was ever more absolute than this natural law upon historical premises. For other systems of natural law gave ideals developed from without. With us, under the dominion of the historical school the sole critique of the law was to be found in the law itself. Moreover, every addition or amendment from without was brought to the same test. As late as 1905 a leader of the American bar, thoroughly imbued with the ideas of the historical school, told us that it was a wise doctrine to presume that legislators intended no innovations upon the common law and to assume so far as possible that statutes were meant to declare and reassert its principles. As no statute of any consequence dealing with any relation of private law can be anything but in derogation of the common law, the social reformer and the legal reformer, under such a doctrine, had always to face the situation that the legislative act which represented the fruit of their labors would find no sympathy in those who applied it, would be construed strictly and would be made to interfere with the *status quo* as little as possible.

Jhering tells a story of a professor to whom a question of commercial law was submitted. He returned an elaborate and thoroughly reasoned answer based upon the principles of the Roman law, the basis of the common law of Continental Europe and hence of legal instruction. Upon suggestion that he had omitted to notice a section of the commercial code which appeared to govern, he responded that if the commercial code saw fit to go counter to reason and the Roman law it was no affair of his. Surely we may sympathize with the learned professor for under the influence of a taught traditional law and of a historical school of jurists which scouts legislative lawmaking we proceed in much the same way. Our text writers will scrupulously gather up from every remote corner the most obsolete decisions and cite them diligently. But they seldom cite any statutes beyond those landmarks which have found a place in our common law. When they do refer to statutes it is almost always solely through judicial decisions in which they are construed or applied. Nor will it do to say that this is justified by the instability of our legislation. Unstable as some of it is, much of it is thoroughly stable while much of our case law is unstable. It is not that the statutes are unstable. It is rather that the reader will not be interested in them. He does not feel that they are law in the same sense as an adjudicated case; he does not want to cite them if a case may be had in which the portions of the statute applicable have been incorporated. Accordingly, it is natural that courts, even where they do not actually hold important legislation to be merely declaratory of the common law, too often make it declaratory in effect by citing prior judicial decisions and assuming that they express the rule enacted by the statute. In this way much of the work of uniform state legislation upon commercial subjects is threatened with undoing.

While the metaphysical jurists were deducing the whole system of rights and the idea of the end of legal systems from a metaphysical conception of liberty, another school of jurists was seeking a practical principle of lawmaking. The metaphysical school was a school of jurists. Its adherents had their eye upon the law as a whole—upon systems which had come down from the past—and they sought the principles upon which such systems and their doctrines might be criticised and their further development might be directed. The English utilitarians, on the other hand, were a school of legislators. While the metaphysical jurists sought principles of criticism of what was, they sought principles of constructing a new body of law. The founder of the utilitarians, Jeremy Bentham, took law reform for his life work. As a practical principle in his work of law reform he took what he called the principle of utility, namely, does the rule or measure conduce to human happiness? His one principle of criticism was, how far does a rule or doctrine or institution conduce to or promote human happiness? This criterion might well have been used to break down the individualist idea of justice. At this time, however, the age of Adam Smith and the great economists, individualist ideas were too firmly fixed in men's minds to be questioned. A criterion of the greatest good of the greatest number possible, of that which serves for the happiness of the greatest number used as the measure of the conduct of each, would not be far from some recent ideas of justice. But Bentham did not question individualism. He vacillated between utility in the sense of the greatest happiness of the individual and in the sense of the greatest happiness of the greatest number. Perhaps as near as he came to a choice was to assume that the greatest general happiness was to be procured through the greatest individual self-assertion. Accordingly his juristic principle was not unlike that of the metaphysical jurists. Everyone, he held, is the best judge of his own happiness. "Hence legislation should aim at a removal of all those restrictions on the free action of an individual which are not necessary for securing the like freedom on the part of his neighbors." It will be seen that practically Bentham's principle was to permit the maximum of free individual action consistent with general free individual action. In effect his conception of the end of the law was the same as that of the metaphysical school—to secure the maximum of abstract individual self-assertion. This fitted entirely with the inherited individualism of common-law lawyers.

Bentham and his immediate disciples believed in legislation. They left their mark upon Anglo-American law through the legislative reform movement of the first half of the last century of which they were the promoters. But this reform movement was not a creative one. In many ways it was analogous to Justinian's legislation in the maturity of Roman law. It carried out to formal and logical fruition ideas which had achieved their maturity in a prior stage of legal development. Bentham's legislation was a pruning away of archaisms, a removal of shackles upon individual activity which had come down from the Middle Ages, and a stating of the law in a more accessible and intelligible form. This conception of legislation coupled with Bentham's interpretation of utility as requiring a minimum of interference with the individual led the next generation of English utilitarians to the same position as that of the historical school. They came to agree that legislation except in emergencies and for certain incidental purposes was an evil. The historical school said it was an evil because it attempted to do what could not be done, namely to make law consciously. The newer utilitarians said it was an evil because that government governed best that left men most free to work out their own happiness. Bentham had already put security as the main end to which the legal order should be directed. Taking this to mean security in the maximum of individual self-assertion a sort of juristic pessimism was developed; a doctrine that we can do no good by law, we may only avert some evils. "Equality," says Markby, one of Bentham's later followers, "may be hindered by the law, it cannot be promoted by it."

In the last two decades of the nineteenth century the juristic ideas on which metaphysical jurist, historical jurist and utilitarian were agreed appeared to be confirmed from a new quarter. Although in common with sociology, sociological jurisprudence has its origin in the positivist philosophers, in the sense that each has a continuous development from Comte's positive philosophy, its development has been determined rather by the social-philosophical school which arose from the breakdown of the metaphysical and historical schools on the Continent. At first, however, the positivist philosophy of law and the so-called sociological science of law were in their way quite as absolute as their rivals. Comte thought of the universe as governed by mathematical mechanical laws, and hence of moral and social phenomena as so governed. The next generation of positivists, influenced by Darwin, thought of evolution as governed by inexorable mechanical laws. Accordingly the positivist or mechanical type of sociologist sought for absolute mechanical social laws whose inevitable operations produced all social, political and jural institutions, as completely apart from human will as the motions of the planets. The positivist jurists sought to find laws of morals and laws of legal and social evolution analogous to gravitation, conservation of energy and the like, and they expected to find these laws through observation and experience. But observation and experience led them to the same result to which metaphysics had led the philosophical jurists and history had led the historical jurists. For one thing, they got their data from the historical jurists and so looked at them not independently but through the metaphysical spectacles of that school. Moreover, like the whole century, they were subconsciously under the influence of Kant. Kant had become a part of the thought of the time so thoroughly that all four of the nineteenth-century schools came to his position as to the end of the law, though for different reasons and in different ways. Thus the views of the positivists were congenial in jurisprudence and were especially congenial in America. Spencer's writings had great vogue in the United States, and many cases where judicial decisions show the effect of his ideas might be cited. Accordingly mechanical sociology lingered in American juristic writing longer than elsewhere because its ideas appeared to confirm those of the historical school. Many who were beginning to be conscious that the historical school could not hold the ground much longer were able to flatter themselves that they were moving forward by giving to their old views a new form of mechanical sociology.

Like the historical jurist, the mechanical sociologist of the end of the nineteenth century looked at law in its evolution, in its successive changes, and sought to relate these changes to changes undergone by society itself. The historical jurist found metaphysical laws behind these changes. The mechanical sociologist substituted physical laws. For all practical purposes the result was the same. This is true especially of the type which has had most vogue in America, namely, the phase of the mechanical sociology which identified with economic laws these supposed mechanical laws which absolutely determine the content of legal systems. It is not too much to say that this combination of the economic interpretation with positivism gave rise to a sort of fatalist natural law. The old natural law called for search for an eternal body of principles to which the positive law must be made to conform. This new natural law called for search for a body of rules governing legal development, to which law will conform do what we may. The operation of these same rules will change it and will change it in accordance with fixed and definite rules in every way comparable to those which determine the events of nature. The most man may do is to observe and thus, it may be, learn to predict. For the rest nature will take her inexorable course and we may but impotently wring our hands. If law is an inevitable resultant, if in making it or finding it, legislator or judge is merely bringing about "conformity to the *de facto* wishes of the dominant forces of the community," conscious effort to improve the law can be effective in appearance only. The eighteenth-century theory, even if it put the basis of legal systems beyond reach of change, moved us to scan the details and to endeavor to make each part conform to the fixed ideal plan. It admitted that legislator and jurist had each a function. The historical school denied any function to the legislator. It said law could no more be made than language. Each was a growth upon the basis of a received tradition. The positivist economic interpretation denied all function to the jurist. To the doctrine of legislative futility, which the historical school had fastened on our teaching, it added a doctrine of juristic futility. It is no wonder that a generation of lawyers trained in nineteenth-century philosophy of law has been slow to respond to the modern faith in the efficacy of effort.

At the end of the last century the rise of the social-philosophical jurists and in the last two decades the development of a sociological jurisprudence which has definitely rejected absolute ideas produced a new legal science on the Continent and its ideas are slowly taking root in Anglo-American thought. But as I shall endeavor to show in a subsequent lecture the good sense of courts has led to a movement beneath the surface in judicial decision which has been in advance of our thinking and teaching. Hence I used to suggest, when the recall was agitating, that our impatient reformers should demand, not recall of judges or of judicial decisions, but recall of law teachers and of juristic thinking. Certainly our busy courts have had much more excuse for being out of touch with recent social and political and economic science when we reflect that everything scientific which was accessible to them in English served to confirm the ideas in which judges had been brought up.

We must recall much of the jurisprudence of the last century. And yet the juristic thought of that time was not wholly in vain. It may teach us that there are inherent limitations on what may be achieved through law and inherent limitations upon the efficacy of effort in conscious lawmaking; that for the greatest part law must always be found through application of reason to causes as they arise and the testing of principles in their actual operation; that laws are not like clothes to be thrown off and replaced at will, but, like language are so intimately a part of all we do that development of the traditional materials will always be the chief agency of growth. Used to temper the enthusiasm of a new period of liberalization, the philosophy of law of the last century may yet save us from the excesses of the stage of equity and natural law, a reaction wherefrom had so much to do with the rigidity of the law under which we live.

VII

JUDICIAL EMPIRICISM

WHEN Tom Sawyer and Huck Finn had determined to rescue Jim by digging under the cabin where he was confined, it seemed to the uninformed lay mind of Huck Finn that some old picks the boys had found were the proper implements to use. But Tom knew better. From reading he knew what was the right course in such cases, and he called for case-knives. "It doesn't make no difference," said Tom, "how foolish it is, it's the *right* way and it's the regular way. And there ain't no other way that I ever heard of, and I've read all the books that gives any information about these things. They always dig out with a case-knife." So in deference to the books and to the proprieties the boys set to work with case-knives. But after they had dug till nearly midnight and they were tired and their hands were blistered and they had made little progress, a light came to Tom's legal mind. He dropped his knife and, turning to Huck, said firmly, "Gimme a case-knife." Let Huck tell the rest:

"He had his own by him, but I handed him mine. He flung it down and says, 'Gimme a *case-knife.*'

"I didn't know just what to do—but then I thought. I scratched around amongst the old tools and got a pickax and give it to him, and he took it and went to work and never said a word.

"He was always just that particular. Full of principle."

Tom Sawyer had made over again one of the earliest discoveries of the law. When legislation or tradition prescribed case-knives for tasks for which pickaxes were better adapted, it seemed better to our forefathers, after a little vain effort with case-knives, to adhere to principle—but use the pickax. They granted that law ought not to change. Changes in law were full of danger. But, on the other hand, it was highly inconvenient to use case-knives. And so the law has always managed to get a pickax in its hands, though it steadfastly demanded a case-knife and to wield it in the virtuous belief that it was using the approved instrument.

It is worth while to recall some of the commonplaces of legal history by way of illustration. One of the first difficulties encountered by archaic legal systems, founded upon the family and postulating for every sort of legal, social and religious institution the continuity of the household, was the failure of issue, the want of the son to perpetuate the household worship whom religious and legal dogmas required. No one thought of superseding these dogmas, but their manifest inconvenience and injustice were avoided by the device of adoption. Presently a better way of disposing of property after death without infringing upon ancient doctrines occurred to some Roman. Why not sell his whole household and estate to the person upon whom he desired it to devolve? If he so sold it and the purchaser was an honorable man, he would carry out oral instructions given at the time of the transfer as to the purpose for which it was made and the disposition to be made of the property. After this had gone on until everyone had begun to employ the proceeding, a law of the Twelve Tables gave legal efficacy to the oral instructions, when the form of sale was had—and wills had come into being. A better example is to be seen in the Roman law of marriage. The religious marriage, which was the only one recognized by religion and hence by law, was not open to the plebeian. In consequence he did not have his wife in *manus* or his children in *potestas* and his household had no standing before the law. The law was not altered. It was not enacted that there might be marriage without a wife in *manus* and a family without children in *potestas,* but purchase or adverse possession and the statute of limitations were resorted to in order to bring the plebeian's wife into *manus* in another way. Our own law furnishes many such instances. When the Anglo-Saxon king desired to extend the protection of his peace to some one, he took him by the hand publicly and made of him, for legal purposes, a minister or servant, entitled to the king's peace which attached to members of his household. When wager of law, a simple oath backed by the oaths of one's neighbors that this oath was clean and unperjured, made the action of debt a worthless action upon simple contracts, wager of law was not abolished but the courts found a trespass and a breach of the king's peace in failure to perform a promise, if only something had been given presently in exchange for it, and thus imposed on our law of contract what has now become the formality of consideration. When the delay and formalism of real actions and the incident of trial by battle made them inadequate remedies, a fictitious lease and fictitious ejectment were resorted to in order to make another remedy meet the situation. When the hard and fast form of writ and declaration failed to provide for new cases of conversion of a plaintiff's property, the form was not altered but a loss and finding were assumed from the conversion, so that we are able to read in an American report of yesterday that the plaintiff casually lost one hundred freight cars and the defendant casually found them and converted them to its own use, as if it were a watch or a pocketbook that had been lost.

Newer and less crude modes of growth were long ago discovered by the law. But this primitive mode of growth by the employment of fictions, which is closely akin to the "let's play" so and so of our childhood, has not disappeared from political institutions. The turning back of the legislative clock is a familiar institution, and in at least one American state, where in an age of printing the constitution requires every bill to be read *in extenso* three times before each house, it is possible today to see five reading clerks simultaneously reading five separate bills, while the legislators peruse their morning papers and answer the letters of their constituents.

After the general employment of fictions has accustomed men to intentional change of law bolder devices come into use. Particular fictions, employed to meet a particular case or to change a particular rule, such as those referred to above, are superseded by what may be called general fictions, fictions having a more sweeping operation to alter or create whole departments of the law, introducing new principles or new methods rather than mere isolated rules. These general fictions are interpretation, equity and natural law.

Interpretation as an agency of growth has to do chiefly with the legislative element. In primitive times, when the law is taken to be God-given and unchangeable, the most that may be permitted to human magistrates is to interpret the sacred text. Later when the customary law has been formulated authoritatively the antipathy of the stage of strict law to change and the desire to limit the judicial function to the purely mechanical in order to insure uniformity leads to an endeavor to confine lawmaking to interpretation and logical development of the text. In the maturity of law the dogma of separation of powers, whereby the making and the application of law are required to be wholly divorced so that judges are to do no more than ascertain the actual intent of the legislator according to settled canons of genuine interpretation, led countries governed by codes to attempt once more to make of the court a mere automaton. As a critic has put it, the theory of the codes in Continental Europe in the last century made of the court a sort of judicial slot machine. The necessary machinery had been provided in advance by legislation or by received legal principles and one had but to put in the facts above and take out the decision below. True, this critic says, the facts do not always fit the machinery, and hence we may have to thump and joggle the machinery a bit in order to get anything out. But even in extreme cases of this departure from the purely automatic, the decision is attributed, not at all to the thumping and joggling process, but solely to the machine. Such a conception of the process of judicial decision cannot stand the critical scrutiny to which all legal and political institutions are now subjected. Men insist upon knowing where the pre-existing rule was to be found before the judges discovered and applied it, in what form it existed, and how and whence it derived its form and obtained its authority. And when as a result of such inquiries, the rule seems to have sprung full fledged from the judicial head, the assumption that the judicial function is one of interpretation and application only leads to the conclusion that the courts are exercising a usurped authority. The true conclusion is, rather, that our political theory of the nature of the judicial function is unsound. It was never truly the common-law theory. In its origin it is a fiction, born in periods of absolute and unchangeable law. If all legal rules are contained in immutable form in holy writ or in twelve tables or in a code or in a received *corpus juris* or in a custom of the realm whose principles are authoritatively evidenced, not only must new situations be met by deduction and analogical extension under the guise of interpretation but the inevitable changes to which all law is subject must be hidden under the same guise. Beginning in this way, the mechanical conception of the judicial office was taken over in political theory through the adoption of the Byzantine idea of sovereignity and consequent reception of the Byzantine notion that the sovereign will both made and interpreted law, and was fixed therein by the general adoption of Montesquieu's theory of the separation of powers. Today, when all recognize, nay insist, that legal systems do and must grow, that legal principles are not absolute, but are relative to time and place, and that juridicial idealism may go no further than the ideals of an epoch, the fiction should be discarded. A process of judicial lawmaking has always gone on and still goes on in all systems of law, no matter how completely in their juristic theory they limit the function of adjudication to the purely mechanical.

In their origin equity and natural law are also general fictions along with interpretation. In our law the chancellor purported to be governed by a body of moral rules of superior sanctity to those of the strict law and to constrain men to perform the moral duties which those rules of equity and good conscience dictated. In the Roman law the jurisconsult held himself bound to take note of certain principles of reason to be found in nature itself by which all matters which he was free to pass upon should be tried and to which all rules which were plastic should be shaped. In each case the result was an infusion of morals into law and a making over of the law, although in theory the old rules stood unaltered. These general fictions, which bore the brunt in past eras of growth, were wholly unsuited to the maturity of law, wherein stability is held the one thing needful, and so fell out of use. Interpretation is the general fiction of the nineteenth century.

Law grows subconsciously at first. Afterwards it grows more or less consciously but as it were surreptitiously under the cloak of fictions. Next it grows consciously but shamefacedly through general fictions. Finally it may grow consciously, deliberately and avowedly through juristic science and legislation tested by judicial empiricism. It is not the least of the achievements of the common law that it discovered and worked out a system of legal development by judicial empiricism at a time when the rest of the world was running to Rome and was seeking to administer justice to modern Europe not by the free judicial methods of the classical jurists but by the hard and fast legislative text and fettered judge of Constantine and Justinian.

A developed legal system is made up of two elements, a traditional or habitual element and an enacted or imperative element. The latter is usually the modern element and at present, so far as the form of the law is concerned, is tending to become predominant. The former is the older or historical element upon which juristic development proceeds by analogy. It is by no means universally true, however, that the imperative element in a legal system is the modern element and the traditional element speaks only from the past. In truth the two act upon and correct each other so that when either, from occupying the field too long, becomes too fixed and rigid, the needed flexibility is restored to the law by its rival. Yet on the whole, the traditional element is by far the more important. In the first instance we must rely upon it to meet all new problems for the legislator acts only after they attract attention. And even after the legislator has acted it is seldom if ever that his foresight extends to all the details of his problem or that he is able to do more than provide a broad if not crude outline. Hence even in the field of the enacted law the traditional element of the legal system plays a chief part. We must rely upon it to fill the gaps in legislation, to develop the principles introduced by legislation, and to interpret them. Let us not forget that so-called interpretation is not merely ascertainment of the legislative intent. If it were it would be the easiest instead of the most difficult of judicial tasks. Where the legislature has had an intent and has sought to express it there is seldom a question of interpretation. The difficulties arise in the myriad cases in respect to which the lawmaker had no intention because he had never thought of them. Indeed perhaps he could never have thought of them. Here, if we insist on the dogmatic separation of powers, the courts, willing or unwilling, must to some extent make the law under the guise of interpretation; and our security that it will be made as law and not as arbitrary will lies in the judicial and juristic tradition from which the materials of judicial lawmaking are derived. Accordingly the traditional element of the legal system is and must be used, even in an age of copious legislation, to supplement, round out and develop the enacted element; and in the end it usually swallows up the latter and incorporates the results in the body of tradition. Moreover a large field is always unappropriated by enactment, and here the traditional element is supreme.

Juristic science works with the materials of the traditional element. It analyzes them and systemizes them, it traces their history, it seeks their philosophical foundations, it compares them with the traditional materials of other legal systems. In this way it prunes away arbitrary rules, molds doctrines into accord with reason and reconciles inconsistencies. In the future, under the influence of the sociological school in jurisprudence, it will add to the foregoing tasks study of the social operation of rules and doctrines and of the effects which they produce in action, in order to determine how far they achieve the ends of law. Legislation on the other hand, except as it merely gives form to what has been worked out by juristic science and stamped with approval by judicial empiricism, has for its function to introduce new premises. In the past, under the influence of absolute ideas of law as something eternal and unchangeable, it took a jural revolution through reversion to justice without law and recourse to some such general fiction as that of equity or natural law to introduce new premises on any considerable scale. Today no such jural revolutions are required. We have come to believe in conscious lawmaking—perhaps, indeed, to have too much faith in what may be achieved thereby. But the true function of codes, as jurists recognize today, is not merely to put the results of past legal development in better and more authoritative form but even more to afford a basis for a juristic and judicial new start. Thus the jurist works over the traditional materials and the legislator provides new materials. From these the judge makes the actual law by a process of trying the principles and rules and standards in concrete cases, observing their practical operation and gradually discovering by experience of many causes how to apply them so as to administer justice by means of them. Such has been the common law from the first. Such is coming to be the accepted theory of the rest of the world as failure of the eighteenth-century attempt to make the courts mere automata leads the jurists of Continental Europe to reject the Byzantine notion of the relation of the judge to the legislator and return to the more liberal doctrine of the classical Roman law.

It was not always the Roman doctrine that law was made only by a legislative act or authentic interpretation by the sovereign. On the contrary in Cicero's time precedents were enumerated among the forms of the law. At the end of the second century a jurist could lay down, on the authority of a rescript, that the authority of cases adjudged to the same effect had the force of law. But Roman case law was made by jurisconsults rather than by judges. For whereas we entrust judicial power to a permanent judge learned in the law but bid him take the facts from a lay jury, the classical Roman polity put the judicial power in the hands of a lay *iudex* chosen for the case in hand and bade him take his law from a duly licensed jurisconsult. Where jurisconsults differed he had to decide what opinion he would adopt. Yet his decision, as that of a layman acting only for the one case, had no particular weight and was not preserved. What was significant was the answer of the learned jurisconsult whose opinion had been sought, and the most enduring part of the Roman law was made up of such opinions. As a permanent judicial magistracy grew up under the empire the function of the jurisconsult waned and it is not unlikely that judicial decisions would have established themselves as a form of law had not the union of all powers, legislative, adminstrative and judicial in the emperors after Diocletian led to the doctrine which Justinian handed down to the modern world with the authoritative stamp of his compilation—the doctrine that the judge can do no more than decide the particular case for the purposes of that case, and that only the sovereign by a legislative act is competent to make a binding rule which shall govern in other cases than that in which it was used as the ground of a decision. In the Middle Ages it was enough that this doctrine had behind it the unassailable authority of Justinian. But when Roman law was first applied by lay judges advised as to the law by learned doctors of the law from the universities, a practice which the trial in Shakespeare's Merchant of Venice may serve to illustrate, it was not to be expected in any event that the decisions of such magistrates could acquire the force of law. The doctrinal writer who furnished the materials for decision was the real voice of the law.

Thus a conception of the judicial office arose on

the Continent which persisted after permanent courts learned in the law had been set up, since it appeared to accord with the theory of the separation of powers and was in line with the political theory which developed in the seventeenth and eighteenth centuries. It was in line also with the eighteenth-century doctrine of a complete code deduced from the principles of natural law. Through the influence of the latter doctrine it became a favorite notion of legislators that the finding of law for the purposes of judicial decision might be reduced to a simple matter of genuine interpretation; that a body of enacted rules might be made so complete and so perfect that the judge would have only to select the one made in advance for the case in hand, find what the lawgiver intended thereby through application of fixed canons of genuine interpretation and proceed to apply it. The code of Frederick the Great was drawn up on this theory. The intention was that "all contingencies should be provided for with such careful minuteness that no possible doubt could arise at any future time. The judges were not to have any discretion as regards interpretation but were to consult a royal commission as to any doubtful points and to be absolutely bound by its answer." "This stereotyping of the law," says Schuster, "was in accordance with the doctrines of the law of nature, according to which a perfect system might be imagined, for which no changes would ever become necessary, and which could, therefore, be laid down once for all, so as to be available for any possible combination of circumstances." So firm a grip has this eighteenth-century doctrine upon American political theory that in 1912 a senator of the United States could tell us complacently that the uncertainties to which judicial construction of the anti-trust laws had led us might be relieved through a bill he had drawn which, he said, "enumerates in plain English every known practice and expedient through which combinations have stifled competition and prohibits anyone from engaging in them." In the same spirit a professor of political science in one of our universities proposed that the power of interpretation should be taken from the courts and be given to some executive body in supposed closer touch with the popular will, confining the courts to the task of applying the prescribed and interpreted rule. Both of these ideas, a complete legislative provision in advance covering every case, and authoritative extra-judicial interpretation, have failed in practice although they have had the advantage of careful, deliberate legislation formulated by experts and of application by bench and bar trained in the Byzantine doctrine. It is as clear as legal history can make it that interpretation apart from judicial application is impracticable; that it is futile to attempt to separate the functions of finding the law, interpreting the law and applying the law. For example, the plan of interpretation by a royal commission, tried in the code of Frederick the Great, failed utterly. It soon appeared that there was no reason for supposing that the executive commission would have more foresight than the legislature. Experience quickly taught that the most which might be achieved in advance was to lay down a premise or a guiding principle and that the details of application must be the product of judicial experiment and judicial experience.

Nevertheless the Byzantine doctrine dies hard. In the nineteenth century certainty was sought not by a complete body of rules covering every case in advance but by a complete body of principles and a complete system of logical exposition and application of those principles. All the nineteenth-century codes in Continental Europe, except the German Civil Code of 1896, go upon the theory that judicial decisions shall have no authority beyond the cases in which they are rendered and that there can be no authoritative interpretation by anyone except the legislature itself. If the codes left anything open, the judges were directed where to turn in order to decide the case. But the next judge was not to look upon the decision of his predecessor as establishing anything. He was to repeat the process independently. An excellent example may be found in article 5 of the French Civil Code. That article reads as follows: "Judges are forbidden, when giving judgment in the cases which are brought before them, to lay down general rules of conduct or decide a case by holding it was governed by a previous decision." Its purpose was, as we are told by an authoritative commentator, to prevent the judges from forming a body of case law which should govern the courts and to prevent them from "correcting by judicial interpretations the mistakes made in the [enacted] law." Before fifty years had passed legislation was required to compel the lower courts to follow the solemn decision of the highest court of France, and now, after a century of experience, French jurists are conceding that the article in question has failed of effect. Today elementary books from which law is taught to the French students, in the face of the code and of the received Roman tradition, do not hesitate to say that the course of judicial decision is a form of law. All over the Continent the new school is clamoring for free judicial finding of law. It is agreed that the path of deliverance from the stagnation of nineteenth-century law is a judicial empiricism, working upon the materials supplied by jurist and legislator.

Anglo-American law is fortunate indeed in entering upon a new period of growth with a well-established doctrine of lawmaking by judicial decision. It is true we have to combat the political theory and the dogma of separation of powers. It is true also that the influence of these ideas and the nineteenth-century insistence upon certainty led to a theory that the judicial finding of law was but a discovery of something which was logically or potentially pre-existing, so that the decision made nothing, it merely evidenced. Undoubtedly under the influence of this idea judicial empiricism was proceeding over-cautiously at the end of the last century. Yet this was not wholly an evil. It would be most unfortunate if both legislature and court should be governed by a conception of law as will and proceed to lay down whatever seemed best, for that reason alone, unrestrained by the necessity of going upon predetermined premises or of developing them by a known technique and along fixed lines. The chief cause of the success of our common-law doctrine of precedents as a form of law is that it combines certainty and power of growth as no other doctrine has been able to do. Certainty is insured within reasonable limits in that the court proceeds by analogy of rules and doctrines in the traditional system and develops a principle for the cause before it according to a known technique. Growth is insured in that the limits of the principle are not fixed authoritatively once for all but are discovered gradually by a process of inclusion and exclusion as cases arise which bring out its practical workings and prove how far it may be made to do justice in its actual operation. If the last century insisted over much upon the predetermined premises and fixed technique, it did not lose to our law the method of applying the judicial experience of the past to the judicial questions of the present and of making that experience yield principles to be developed into working and workable rules of justice by a process of judicial experimentation.

There is a common element in the two fundamental doctrines of the common law, the doctrine of precedents and the doctrine of the supremacy of law. The same spirit is behind each. The doctrine of precedents means that causes are to be judged by principles reached inductively from the judicial experience of the past, not by deduction from rules established arbitrarily by the sovereign will. In other words, reason, not arbitrary will is to be the ultimate ground of decision. The doctrine of supremacy of law is reducible to the same idea. It is a doctrine that the sovereign and all its agencies are bound to act upon principles, not according to arbitrary will; are obliged to follow reason instead of being free to follow caprice. Both represent the Germanic idea of law as a quest for the justice and truth of the Creator. The common-law doctrine is one of reason applied to experience. It assumes that experience will afford the most satisfactory foundation for standards of action and principles of decision. It holds that law is not to be made arbitrarily by a fiat of the sovereign will, but is to be discovered by judicial and juristic experience of the rules and principles which in the past have accomplished or have failed to accomplish justice. Where such a doctrine obtains, not merely the interpretation and application of legal rules but in large measure the ascertainment of them must be left to the disciplined reason of the judges, and we must find in the criticism of the reported decision by bench and bar in other cases our assurance that they will be governed by reason and that the personal equation of the individual judge will be suppressed. The vitality of the common law and the steady increase in the value attributed to judicial decisions in the rest of the world attest the soundness of this expectation. We have, then, the means of progress in our law to begin with, where the rest of the world is struggling to attain it. It is the part of wisdom to preserve and develop it and to set up and maintain courts adequate to employ it instead of experimenting with the Byzantine doctrine which has been thoroughly tried and found wanting in Continental Europe or with the Byzantine method of administration in any of its forms.

Much of the criticism of our Anglo-American system of judicial empiricism assumes that it is responsible for the obstinacy with which American law stood in its tracks at the end of the last century while other departments of human endeavor were moving on. But it must be remembered that American law was not alone in this respect. The world over the law of the last century sought to stand still, and the century demanded that it do so. No matter what the form of the law, code or case law or received Roman tradition modernized and made a juristic tradition, we see the same characteristic condition of quiescence.

If the causes of the backwardness of the law with respect to social problems and the unsocial attitude of the law toward questions of great import in the modern community are to be found in the traditional element of our legal system, determined by a succession of causes which I have discussed in the preceding lectures, the surest means of deliverance are to be found there also. The infusion of morals into the law through the development of equity was not an achievement of legislation, it was the work of courts. The absorption of the usages of merchants into the law was not brought about by statutes but by judicial decisions. When once the current of juristic thought and judicial decision is turned into the new course our Anglo-American method of judicial empiricism has always proved adequate. Given new premises, our common law has the means of developing them to meet the exigencies of justice and of molding the results into a scientific system. Moreover it has the power of acquiring new premises, as it did in the development of equity and the absorption of the law merchant. Indeed fundamental changes have been taking place in our legal system almost unnoticed, and a shifting was in progress in our case law from the individualist justice of the nineteenth century, which has passed so significantly by the name of legal justice, to the social justice of today even before the change in our legislative policy became so marked.

Eight noteworthy changes in the law in the present generation, which are in the spirit of recent ethics, recent philosophy and recent political thought, will serve to make the point.

First among these we may note limitations on the use of property, attempts to prevent anti-social exercise of the incidents of ownership. At this point judicial decision has been the agency of progress. This is no time or place for details. I need only refer to the gradual but steady change of front in our case law with respect to the so-called spite fence, and to the establishment in American case law of doctrines with respect to percolating water and to surface water, in which a principle of reasonable use has superseded the old and narrow idea that the owner of the surface might do as he pleased. In this growing tendency of the law to impose limitations on the use of property, especially limitations designed to prevent what the French call "abusive exercise of rights," there is a suggestive parallel between the period of legal development on which we have entered and the earlier period of liberalization which I have called the stage of equity or natural law. Equity sought to prevent the unconscientious exercise of legal rights; today we seek to prevent the anti-social exercise of them. Equity imposed moral limitations; the law of today is imposing social limitations. It is endeavoring to delimit the individual interest better with respect to social interests and to confine the legal right to the bounds of the interest so delimited. More and more the tendency is to hold that what the law should secure is satisfaction of the owner's reasonable wants with respect to the property—that is those which consist with the like wants of his neighbors and the interests of society.

Second, we may note limitations upon freedom of contract. Such limitations have been imposed both through legislation and through judicial decision. As examples of legislative limitations reference may be made to statutes requiring payment of wages in cash, statutes regulating conditions of labor, and legislation with respect to non-living wage, minimum wage and the like. As examples of judicial limitations, it is enough to remind you that our courts have taken the law of insurance practically out of the category of contract, have taken the law of surety companies practically out of the law of suretyship and have established that the duties of public service companies are not contractual, flowing from agreement, but instead flow from the calling in which the public servant is engaged. Here again the parallel between the present and the stage of equity or natural law is suggestive. Equity sought by limiting their power of contract to protect debtors against unfair advantage on the part of creditors. Accordingly it prevented clogs upon or bargainings away of the debtor's right to redeem mortgaged property and overturned oppressive contracts with heirs and reversioners. Today we seek once more, by limiting freedom of contract, to protect those who are subjected to economic pressure against unfair advantage on the part of those who have greater economic freedom.

Third, we may note limitations on the power of disposing of property. These are chiefly legislative. Examples are the requirement in many states that the wife join in a conveyance of the family home; the statutes in some jurisdictions requiring the wife to join in a mortgage of household goods; the statute of Massachusetts requiring the wife to join in an assignment of the husband's wages. But there has been a tendency in judicial decision to put limitations on the *jus disponendi* in order to prevent acquisition or perpetuation of a monopoly by unfair underselling in particular localities.

Fourth, reference may be made to limitations upon the power of the creditor or injured party to secure satisfaction. The Roman law in its classical period had developed something of this sort. In the case of certain debtors as against certain creditors the Roman law gave the benefit or the privilege of not answering for the entire amount but for so much as the debtor could pay for the time being. Naturally this doctrine was rejected in the modern civil law as being out of accord with the individualism of the eighteenth and nineteenth centuries. The newer codes, however, have a number of provisions restricting the power of the creditor to secure satisfaction, such as, for example, provision that the statutory liability of an insane wrongdoer shall not go so far as to deprive him of means of support. In the United States the homestead exemption statutes which prevail in so many states, and the personalty exemptions which in some states go so far as to exempt five hundred dollars to the head of the family, and usually make liberal exemptions of tools to the artisan, library to the professional man, animals and implements to the farmer, and wages to the head of a family, will serve as illustrations. There is a notable tendency in recent legislation and in recent discussion to insist not that the debtor keep faith in all cases even if it ruin him and his family, but that the creditor must take a risk also—either along with or even in some cases instead of the debtor.

Fifth, there is a tendency to revive the idea of liability without fault not only in the form of wide responsibility for agencies employed, but in placing upon an enterprise the burden of repairing injuries, without fault of him who conducts it, which are incident to the undertaking. What Dean Ames, from the standpoint of the historical jurist reviewing the gradual development of legal doctrines based upon free action of the human will, called "the unmoral standard of acting at one's peril" is coming back into the law. There is a strong and growing tendency, where there is no blame on either side, to ask in view of the exigencies of social justice, who can best bear the loss.

Sixth, there is a very marked tendency in judicial decision to regard the social interest in the use and conservation of natural resources; to hold, for example, that running water and wild game are, as it were, assets of society which are not capable of private appropriation or ownership except under regulations that protect the social interest.

Seventh, we may note an increasing tendency to hold that public funds should respond for injuries to individuals by public agencies; that the risk of injuries to individuals inherent in the operations of government are not to be borne exclusively by the luckless individual on whom loss happens to fall.

Finally, recent legislation and judicial decision have changed the old attitude of the law with respect to dependent members of the household. Courts no longer make the natural rights of parents with respect to children the chief basis of their decisions. The individual interest of parents which used to be the one thing regarded has come to be almost the last thing regarded as compared with the interest of the child and the interest of society. In other words, here also social interests are now chiefly regarded.

It is true many of the examples I have just adduced are taken from legislation. It is true also that some of these legislative innovations upon the settled legal ideas of the past two centuries have been resisted bitterly by some courts. Yet I am confident that every one of them would stand in the highest court of the land and in a growing majority of our state courts today. Moreover, what is more important, many of the most significant examples are taken from judicial decisions. If, therefore, the disease is in the traditional element of our legal system, the cure is going on there under our eyes. It is an infusion of social ideas into the traditional element of our law that we must bring about; and such an infusion is going on. The right course is not to tinker with our courts and with our judicial organization in the hope of bringing about particular results in particular kinds of cases at a sacrifice of all that we have learned or ought to have learned from legal and judicial history. It is rather to provide a new set of premises, a new order of ideas in such form that the courts may use them and develop them into a modern system by judicial experience of actual causes. A body of law which will satisfy the demands of the society of today cannot be made of the ultra-individualist materials of eighteenth-century jurisprudence and nineteenth-century common law based thereon, no matter how judges are chosen or how often they are dismissed. For a great part the way must be prepared by juristic science and by careful legislation worked out consistently and upon a clear program, as the legislation of the reform movement in the first half of the nineteenth century was framed on the basis of Bentham's doctrine of utility.

In reason the judges may not be asked to lead in the present transition. They must go with the main body not with the advance guard, and with the main body only when it has attained reasonably fixed and settled conceptions. Let us remember that it is not so long ago that the votaries of the social sciences who now complain of law had succeeded in confirming lawyers in the ideas they had found in their law books. They cannot expect courts, which have the whole economic structure in their hands and are bound to regard the social interest in general security, to turn the law about in a moment. When we reflect how fundamental is the shifting from the older idea of the end of the legal order to the newer, how uncertain the new lines are as yet on the one hand, and on the other hand how completely the change goes to the root of everything the courts do, we must recognize how futile it is to expect the courts to adjust our whole legal system to it over night.

Lay bad-men interpretations are superficial. The fundamental difference between the law of the nineteenth century and the law of the period of legal development on which we have entered is not in the least due to the dominance of sinister interests over courts or lawyers or jurists. It is not due, the legal muckraker notwithstanding, to bad men in judicial office or to intentional enemies to society in high places at the bar. It is a conflict of ideas, not of men; a clash between conceptions that have come down to us and entered into the very flesh and blood of our institutions and modern juristic conceptions born of a new movement in all the social sciences.

Study of fundamental problems, not reversion to justice without law through changes in the judicial establishment or referenda on judicial decisions, is the road to socialization of the law.

VIII

LEGAL REASON

WILLIAM JAMES tells a story, which he attributes to the Danish philosopher Höffding, about a small boy who asked his mother if it were really true that God had made the whole world in six days. "Oh yes," she answered, "it was quite true." "Did he make it *all* in six days," asked the boy? "Oh yes," she said, "it's all done." "Well then," said he, "mamma, what is God doing now?" Höffding considered that the mother ought to have explained to him that God was now sitting for His portrait to the metaphysicians. In truth all attempt to give a philosophical account of some section of recorded human conduct is on a smaller scale very like the attempt of the professional philosopher to make God sit for His portrait. Moreover, if we are to make an adequate picture of a stage of legal development, the picture must be taken after the period has definitely come to an end so that we may view its phenomena, as it were, under the aspect of eternity. It is, therefore, a rash undertaking to essay even a snapshot photograph of the stage of legal development into which we are passing. But without some such attempt we shall fail to understand one of the chief instruments by which the traditional materials of our legal system are kept in touch with reality and are made available for a changed and changing society.

In a former lecture I sought to show that the process of judicial lawmaking consisted in development of the materials of the common-law tradition and of the new premises provided, largely on the basis of that tradition by jurist and legislator, by means of a known technique—the "artificial reason and judgment of the law" of which Lord Coke told his indignant sovereign. For whether working upon the materials of the tradition with the case-knife or pickax of the beginnings of legal science or with the more complicated instruments of the modern legal armory, judicial activity must be directed consciously or unconsciously to some end. In the beginnings of law this end was simply a peaceable ordering. In Roman law and in the Middle Ages it was the maintenance of the social *status quo*. From the seventeenth century until our own day it has been the promotion of a maximum of individual self-assertion. Assuming some one of these as the end of the legal ordering of society, the jurist works out an elaborate critique on the basis thereof, the legislator provides new premises for judicial decision more or less expressing the principles of this critique, and the judge applies it in his choice of analogies when called upon to deal with questions of first impression and uses it to measure existing rules or doctrines in passing upon variant states of fact and thus to shape these rules and doctrines by extending or limiting them in different directions. The basis of all these operations is some theory as to what law is for. When, then, is the theory of the new stage of legal development upon which we seem to be entering?

Those who conceive that the law is entering upon such a new stage of development—and this category includes the professor of jurisprudence at as conservative an institution as the University of Oxford—speak of that stage, in contrast with the nineteenth century, as a stage of socialization of law. For in contrast with the nineteenth century it appears to put the emphasis upon social interests; upon the demands or claims or desires involved in social life rather than upon the qualities of the abstract man *in vacuo* or upon the freedom of will of the isolated individual. But if the term "socialization of law" has alarming implications for any of you, if like the Russian censor who blocked out the words "dynamic" and "sociology" in Ward's Dynamic Sociology wherever they occurred—not that he knew what they meant, but because they sounded too suspiciously like dynamite and socialism—or like the president of one of our universities to whom the word sociological, when used in connection with jurisprudence suggests a professorial masseur massaging a *corpus juris* which is safe only in the hands of regular practitioners—if like either of these you are in fear of mere names, it is possible to put the matter in wholly innocuous phrases and in terms of the modes of thought of the moment. Let us put the new point of view in terms of engineering; let us speak of a change from a political or ethical idealistic interpretation to an engineering interpretation. Let us think of the problem of the end of law in terms of a great task or great series of tasks of social engineering. Let us say that the change consists in thinking not of an abstract harmonizing of human wills but of a concrete securing or realizing of human interests. From an earthly standpoint the central tragedy of existence is that there are not enough of the material goods of existence, as it were, to go round; that while individual claims and wants and desires are infinite, the material means of satisfying them are finite; that while, in common phrase, we all want the earth, there are many of us but there is only one earth. Thus we may think of the task of the legal order as one of precluding friction and eliminating waste; as one of conserving the goods of existence in order to make them go as far as possible, and of precluding friction and eliminating waste in the human use and enjoyment of them, so that where each may not have all that he claims, he may at least have all that is possible. Put in this way, we are seeking to secure as much of human claims and desires—that is as much of the whole scheme of interests—as possible, with the least sacrifice of such interests. Let us apply this engineering interpretation to the eight phenomena in American law of the present of which I spoke in the last lecture.

First we noted the growth of limitations on the use of property, of limitations on exercise of the incidents of ownership. To the nineteenth-century way of thinking the question was simply one of the right of the owner and of the right of his neighbor. Within his physical boundaries the dominion of each was complete. So long as he kept within them and what he did within them was consistent with an equally absolute dominion of the neighbor within his boundaries, the law was to keep its hands off. For the end of law was taken to be a maximum of self-assertion by each, limited only by the possibility of a like self-assertion by all. If, therefore, he built a fence eight feet high cutting off light and air from his neighbor and painted the fence on the side toward his neighbor in stripes of hideous colors, this was consistent with his neighbor's doing the same; it was an exercise of his incidental *jus utendi,* and the mere circumstance that he did it out of unmixed malice was quite immaterial since it in no way infringed the liberty or invaded the property of the neighbor. But suppose we think of law not negatively as a system of hands off while individuals assert themselves freely, but positively as a social institution existing for social ends. Thinking thus, what claims or demands or wants of society are involved in such a controversy? There is an individual interest of substance on the part of each. Each asserts a claim to use, enjoy and get the benefit of the land of which the law recognizes him as the owner. Also the one asserts an individual interest of personality, a claim to exert his will and exercise his faculties freely and hence to employ them in such building operations upon his land as he thinks proper. What shall society say to these claims? If we think in terms of social interests and of giving effect to individual claims to the extent that they coincide with or may be identified with a social interest, we shall say that there is a social interest in the security of acquisitions, on which our economic order rests, and a social interest in the individual life. But that security of acquisitions is satisfied by use of property for the satisfaction of wants of the owner which are consistent with social life; or at least it is not seriously impaired by so limiting it in order to give effect to other wants which are consistent with social life. And the individual life, in which there is a social interest, is a moral and social life. Hence the social interest does not extend to exercise of individual faculties for anti-social purposes of gratifying malice. The moment we put the matter in terms of social life rather than of abstract individual will, we come to the result to which the law has been coming more and more of late throughout the world.

Take our second case, the rise of limitations upon freedom of contract. In a case of 1886, which was the starting point of a long line of cases in the last century, a mining company paid wages in orders on a company store. The legislature forbade this, and the question was whether the statute forbidding it and enacting that persons employing more than a certain number of employees should pay wages in cash was an arbitrary interference with free contract, an unreasonable restriction of the power of free men to make such contracts as they pleased, and so unconstitutional and void. Looking at the matter simply as between the abstract individual mining operator and the abstract individual miner, and this was the way in which the nineteenth century looked at such things, we should probably say something like the following: The legislative restriction does not promote a maximum of free individual self-assertion but on the contrary restrains such self-assertion and does not do this in order that others may have a like freedom of self-assertion. Hence it is an unjustifiable interference with a natural right. And this is exactly what the court said in the actual case. But suppose we think in terms of the interest of society in the individual moral and social life, the interest of society in the human life of the individuals therein. It is no infringement of the human dignity and no considerable interference with the full human life of the operator to say to him that he shall pay wages only in cash, while only by some compromise of conflicting claims which imposes such a limitation may we secure the human dignity of the employees and enable them to live human lives in a civilized society. The criterion actually employed is the one proposed by William James as a principle of ethical philosophy—"since all demands conjointly cannot be satisfied in this poor world," our aim should be "to satisfy as many as we can with the least sacrifice of other demands." Tried by a social-utilitarian criterion of securing as many interests or as much of interests as we may with the least sacrifice of other interests, the restriction upon free contract is justified, and the courts of today have come to that conclusion.

Turn now to the third case, namely, imposition of limitations upon the power of an owner to dispose of property. A husband earns one hundred dollars in wages and is about to assign this product of his toil to a "loan shark." The legislature steps in and says to him: You shall not exercise this incident of your ownership of this claim for wages unless your wife is willing to join in the assignment. The nineteenth century would have thought at once of an abstract free man of full age and sound mind, possessed of a claim for wages as part of his substance, and would have asked: How does this restriction of the power of the owner of a claim to assign it promote a maximum of abstract individual free self-assertion? Is such a restriction in any way required to secure some liberty to all by which we may justify restraint of the liberty of this one? The answer must be in the negative, and if such a statute had been enacted in the eighties of the last century instead of the second decade of the present century, it would have fared hard in the courts. But let us look at it from the standpoint of the social interests involved. The husband's claim is to be subsumed under a social interest in the security of acquisitions, the wife's under a social interest in the security of domestic institutions, the chiefest of social institutions. The infringement of the general security of acquisitions involved in such a restriction is negligible. The control of men in general over their property is scarcely affected thereby. On the other hand the most important of social institutions is secured and protected against practices that sorely threaten its existence in crowded, urban, industrial communities.

Or take the limitations upon the power of creditors to exact satisfaction which have become so common and were denounced so extravagantly by courts when first they were enacted. These courts thought wholly in terms of an abstract individual debtor and an abstract individual creditor, and so the case against such restrictions seemed simple and clear.

But if we ask how far we may trench upon the social interest in the security of transactions, a fundamental form of the general security in a commercial and industrial society based upon credit—if we ask how far we may impair this interest to secure the social interest in the individual life to the extent of preserving a minimum human life to the debtor, our question becomes one of a compromise that will secure as much as possible of each with the least sacrifice of either, and we obtain a rational basis for legislation which when enacted more or less on instinct in the immediate past, has been governed too often merely by sentiment or by pressure from class-conscious persons "actually engaged in the business of agriculture."

Just now few things excite more vigorous judicial dissent than new examples of the notable tendency in recent decision and in recent legislation to impose liability in the absence of fault. A minority of the highest court in the land see in decisions upholding legislative imposition of such liability "a menace to all rights, subjecting them unreservedly to considerations of policy." But new cases are adding continually. Let us take an example from legislation. In more than one jurisdiction if the owner of an automobile allows the machine to go out upon the highway in control of a person who is not licensed to operate a car he is liable at his peril both penally and in damages if some injury occurs, although he is wholly free from want of care and has taken all reasonable precautions. If an unauthorized person took the machine out without his knowledge he is none the less held to answer for resulting injuries. How may we justify the imposition of such a liability? If we think only in terms of the individual owner and the individual pedestrian who is run over it is not easy to do so. But if we think on the one hand of the security of acquisitions and the individual life of the owner, with its incident of free exercise of his faculties by owning a car, and on the other hand of the general security of life and limb, and ask what rule will secure the most with the least sacrifice, the matter looks very different. The whole course of the law today is palpably a result of the latter way of looking at such questions.

Another change in the judicial and legislative attitude in the last thirty years has taken the form of change of *res communes* and *res nullius* into *res publicæ*. As we used to think, certain things were *res communes*. Although, following the language of Roman law they were said to be incapable of ownership by any one and their use was said to be common to all, we had come to think rather of individual rights of using these things and of the persons in whom these rights resided. The law ascertained the persons who might use these things, attributed to them individual rights of property and fixed the extent of such rights. Other things were *res nullius*. No one owned them for the time being, but any one who took possession of them intending to make them his own might become owner by so doing. Of late there has been an increasing tendency to treat both as *res publicæ;* to hold, as some have put it, that both are "owned by the state in trust for the people"; to hold that conservation and socially advantageous use of these things, regarded as natural resources of society, requires that no one be suffered to acquire any property in them or any property right in the use of them, but that they be administered by the state so as to secure the largest and widest and most beneficial use of them consistent with conserving them. Here the social interest in the conservation of natural resources has come to be recognized and a compromise is sought not between the wills of conflicting individual claimants to control over them but between the exigencies of that interest and those of the interest in free exercise of individual powers and the interest in security of acquisitions.

But enough of these illustrations. For by this time you will have perceived the method. The jurisprudence of today catalogues or inventories individual claims, individual wants, individual desires, as did the jurisprudence of the nineteenth century. Only it does not stop there and assume that these claims inevitably call for legal recognition and legal securing in and of themselves. It goes on to ask: What claims, what demands are involved in the existence of the society in which these individual demands are put forward; how far may these individual demands be put in terms of those social interests or identified with them, and when so subsumed under social interests, in so far as they may be so treated, what will give the fullest effect to those social interests with the least sacrifice? We owe this way of thinking to Rudolf von Jhering who was the first to insist upon the interests which the legal order secures rather than the legal rights by which it secures them.

Law begins by granting remedies; by allowing actions. In time we generalize from these actions and perceive rights behind them. But as the actions are means for vindicating rights, so the rights are means conferred by law for securing the interests which it recognizes. Accordingly the scheme of natural rights, to be secured at all hazards, becomes a scheme of interests—of human claims or wants or demands—which we may think the law ought to protect and secure so far as they may be protected and secured; it becomes something for the lawmaker to take account of as of moral and political significance rather than something for the judge to consider as of *legal* significance. As was pointed out in the lecture on the philosophy of law in the nineteenth century, prior to Jhering all theories of law were individualist. The purpose of law was held to be a harmonizing of individual wills in such a way as to leave to each the greatest possible scope for free action. Such, we saw, was the view both of philosophical and of historical jurists. On the other hand, Jhering's is a social theory of law. Whereas the eighteenth century conceived of law as something which the individual invoked against society, the idea of our American bills of rights, Jhering taught that it was something created by society, through which the individual found a means of securing his interests, so far as society recognized them. Although much ingenious philosophical criticism has been directed against this theory, it has not affected the central point. The conception of law as a securing of interests or a protecting of relations has all but universally superseded the individualist theory.

Jhering's work is of enduring value for legal science. The older juristic theory of law as a means to individual liberty and of laws as limitations upon individual wills to secure individual liberty, divorced the jurist from the actual life of today. The jurists of whom Jhering made fun, translated to a heaven of juristic conceptions and seated before a machine which brought out of each conception its nine hundred and ninety-nine thousand nine hundred and ninety-nine logical results, have their counterpart in American judges of the end of the last century who insisted upon a legal theory of equality of rights and liberty of contract in the face of notorious social and economic facts. On the other hand, the conception of law as a means toward social ends, the doctrine that law exists to secure interests, social, public and individual, requires the jurist to keep in touch with life. Wholly abstract considerations do not suffice to justify legal rules under such a theory. The function of legal history comes to be one of illustrating how rules and principles have met concrete situations in the past and of enabling us to judge how we may deal with such situations in the present rather than one of furnishing self-sufficient premises from which rules are to be obtained by rigid deduction.

Three features of this social utilitarianism are significant for our task of shaping the materials of the common-law tradition to meet the purposes of today and of tomorrow. One is the light which it throws on legal history. Nineteenth-century individualism wrote legal history as the record of a continually strengthening and increasing securing of the logical deductions from individual freedom in the form of individual rights, and hence as a product of the pressure of individual claims or wants or desires. But this is just what it is not. It is not too much to say that the social interest in the general security, in its lowest terms of an interest in peace and order, dictated the very beginnings of law. Take, for example, the truce or peace, the most fruitful of the institutions of Germanic law. As we find this institution in Anglo-Saxon law, one type comprises the church peace and the peace of festivals and holydays—the exemption of the church and of these days from prosecution of the feud or seeking of redress by means of private war. What is behind this exemption, the pressure of individual interests calling for public recognition and security or the social interest in social performance of the duties of religion in a Christian society? Another type comprises the peace of the walled town to which the country people had fled when the kingdom was invaded and the peace of the time when the king summoned the host to gather under his leadership in event of war. Here also the feud and private vengeance were suspended. Why? Is it because of the pressure of individual wants taking form in recognition of individual rights, or is it because of a social interest in the performance of military duties essential to maintenance of society, to which the individual claims to redress must for the time being give way? Still another type comprises the peace of the market, the peace of forest and the peace of the great highways. These places also were exempted from violent prosecution of claims to redress. Is it not clear that the basis of this exemption is to be found not in the pressure of individual interests but in the social interest in the social performance of the economic functions on which society rested? Again the peace of the *gemot* or assembly of the free men for political and judicial purposes rests upon the social interest in the unimpeded functioning of the political instiutions by which the social order was maintained, and, without going into more detail, the other phases of the truce or peace are expressions or recognitions of the paramount social interest in the general security.

Secondly, from a social-utilitarian standpoint the history of law is a record of continually wider recognition and more efficacious securing of social interests. This may be seen in the development of legal rules and doctrines, but it appears also in the development of juristic thought as to the end of the legal order. Hippodamus of Miletus, a writer on law and politics in the fifth century B. C., proposed a threefold classification of law because, he said, there were but three possible subjects of legal proceedings, namely, insult, injury and homicide. In this statement of the scope of law the general security is the only interest taken into account and only the simplest phases of that interest are regarded. More than a thousand years later the Institutes of Justinian sought to reduce the whole law to three precepts:

To live honorably, not to injure another, and to give to each his own. In this statement of the scope and subject matter of law the general security is conceived more widely, the security of acquisitions is recognized as such, and a social interest in the general morals is added. Still a thousand years later Bacon, if indeed the treatise on the Use of the Law is his, could not find as much as this in the English law of the sixteenth century. He put the ends of the legal order as three: To secure us in property, to secure us in life and to secure us in our reputations. Here the general security is conceived narrowly in terms of individual substance and of individual personality in the two simple forms of life and reputation. In the nineteenth century Bentham stated the ends of law as four: To provide subsistence, to maintain security, to promote abundance and to favor equality. Here the second of the four includes two of Justinian's three and much besides.

But even Bentham's comprehensive statement is inadequate to the multitude of claims which the law of today recognizes and seeks to secure. For if we look only at social interests, we may see that the legal order endeavors to give effect to at least six groups of claims or demands involved in the existence of civilized society. First we may put the general security, the claim or want of civilized society to be secure from those acts or courses of conduct that threaten its existence. This paramount social interest includes (1) peace and order, the first interest to receive legal recognition, (2) the general health, recognition whereof by means of sanitary legislation was objected to by the positivists a generation ago, (3) the security of acquisitions and (4) the security of transactions. The security of acquisitions was recognized in Justinian's three precepts and has been emphasized ever since. The security of transactions is no less important in an economic order resting upon credit, and the last century insisted upon these two phases of the general security at the expense of the individual life. Second, there is the security of social institutions, the claim or want of civilized society to be secure from those acts or courses of conduct which threaten or impede the functioning of its fundamental institutions, domestic, religious and political. Third, we may put the conservation of social resources, the claim or want of civilized society that the natural media of civilized human existence and means of satisfying human wants in such a society shall not be wasted and shall be used and enjoyed in a manner consistent with the widest and most beneficial application of them to human purposes. In a world of discovery and colonizing activity, in a society of pioneers engaged in discovering, appropriating and exploiting the resources of nature, this interest seemed negligible. In the crowded world of today the law is constantly taking account of it and the *jus abutendi* as an incident of ownership is becoming obsolete. Fourth we may put the general morals, the claim or want of civilized society to be secure against those acts and courses of conduct which run counter to the moral sentiment of the general body of those who live therein for the time being. In primitive society this interest is secured through organized religion. But the law soon takes it over. In our law today it is secured through the common law as to misdemeanors, by definition of a multitude of statutory offences and by the doctrine of a public policy against things of immoral tendency. Fifth there is the interest in general progress, the claim or want of civilized society to be secure against those acts and courses of conduct that interfere with economic, political and cultural progress and the claim that so far as possible individual conduct be so shaped as to conduce to these forms of progress. The law is coming to be full of recognitions of this interest. Lastly, sixth, we may put the social interest in the individual human life, the claim or want of civilized society that each individual therein be able to live a human life according to the standards of the society, and to be secure against those acts and courses of conduct which interfere with the possibility of each individual's living such a life. Recognition of this interest as such is characteristic of the law of the present and the twentieth century is insisting upon it as strongly as the seventeenth century insisted upon the general morals or the nineteenth century upon the security of acquisitions and the security of transactions.

Finally as a result of social utilitarianism the legal reason of today in shaping rules and developing traditional premises of the legal system in order to give effect to social interests, looks at them in terms of the concrete situation, not in terms of the abstract claims of abstract human beings. The purely abstract legal reason of the nineteenth century was set forth satirically by an English judge who, in the old days before the divorce court, was called on to sentence a workingman convicted of bigamy. On being asked what he had to say why sentence should not be pronounced, the accused told a moving story of how his wife had run away with another man and left him with a number of small children to look after while barely earning a living by hard labor. After waiting several years he remarried in order to provide a proper home for the children. Mr. Justice Maule shook his head. "My good man," said he, "the law did not in any wise leave you without a sufficient remedy. You should first have brought an action in Her Majesty's Court of Common Pleas against this man with whom, as you say, your wife went away. In that action, after two or three years and the expenditure of two or three hundred pounds you would have obtained a judgment against him which very likely would have been uncollectible. You should then have brought a suit against your wife in the ecclesiastical court for a divorce from bed and board, which you might have obtained in two or three years after expenditure of two or three hundred pounds. You would then have been able to apply to Parliament for an absolute divorce, which you might have obtained in four or five years more after spending four or five hundred pounds. And," he continued, for he saw the accused impatiently seeking to interpose and to say something, "if you tell me that you never had and never in your life expect to have so many pennies at one time, my answer must be that it hath ever been the glory of England not to have one law for the rich and another for the poor." Accordingly, he imposed a sentence of imprisonment for one day. But Maule, J., was ahead of his time. Even down to the end of the last century, lawyers took seriously the existence of theoretical remedies which in practice were unavailable and regarded the abstract justice of abstract rules as quite enough, be the concrete results what they might. This attitude was a natural result of measuring the law solely by standards drawn from the law itself.

In the past century we studied law from within. The jurists of today are studying it from without. The past century sought to develop completely and harmoniously the fundamental principles which jurists discovered by metaphysics or by history. The jurists of today seek to enable and to compel lawmaking and also the interpretation and application of legal rules, to take more account and more intelligent account, of the social facts upon which law must proceed and to which it is to be applied. Where the last century studied law in the abstract, they insist upon study of the actual social effects of legal institutions and legal doctrines. Where the last century prepared for legislation by study of other legislation analytically, they insist on sociological study in connection with legal study in preparation for legislation. Where the last century held comparative law the best foundation for wise lawmaking, they hold it not enough to compare the laws themselves, but that even more their social operation must be studied and the effects which they produce, if any, when put in action. Where the last century studied only the making of law, they hold it necessary to study as well the means of making legal rules effective. Where the last century made of legal history merely a study of how doctrines have evolved and developed considered solely as jural materials, they call for a sociological legal history, a study of the social effects which the doctrines of the law have produced in the past and of how they have produced them. They call for a legal history which shall not deal with rules and doctrines apart from the economic and social history of their time, as if the causes of change in the law were always to be found in the legal phenomena of the past; a legal history that shall not try to show that the law of the past can give us an answer to every question by systematic deduction as if it were a system without hiatus and without antinomies. They call for a legal history which is to show us how the law of the past grew out of social, economic and psychological conditions, how it accommodated itself to them, and how far we may proceed upon that law as a basis, or in disregard of it, with well-grounded expectations of producing the results desired. In these ways they strive to make effort more effective in achieving the purposes of law. Such is the spirit of twentieth-century jurisprudence. Such is the spirit in which legal reason is to be employed upon our received jural materials in order to make of them instruments for realizing justice in the world of today.

But a new theory of lawmaking as a social function is not the whole of our task. Before we can have sound theories here we need facts on which to build them. Even after we get sound theories, we shall need facts to enable us to apply them. Hard as it is for legislators to ascertain social facts, it is even more difficult for courts with the machinery which our judicial organization affords. As a general proposition, courts have no adequate machinery for getting at the facts required for the exercise of their necessary lawmaking function. As things are, our courts must decide on the basis of matters of general knowledge and on supposed accepted principles of uniform application. Except as counsel furnish material in their printed arguments, a court has no facilities for obtaining knowledge of social facts comparable to hearings before committees, testimony of specialists who have conducted detailed investigations, and other means of the sort available to the legislature. Yet judges must make law as well as apply it, and judicial reference bureaus not remotely unlike Dr. McCarthy's epoch-making contribution to practical legislative lawmaking are not unlikely to develop. The laboratories and staffs of experts which are coming to be attached to some tribunals strongly suggest this. But before we can do anything in this direction, we must provide a more flexible judicial organization. We must give our courts power to organize such administrative agencies as the business before them may require. The present system, in which in many of our jurisdictions the judges are at the mercy of elective administrative officers over whom they have no control, is incompatible with effective handling of social facts in our tribunals. We must abandon to some extent the hard and fast line between the judicial and the administrative involved in our legal tradition. We must recognize that not a little of the administrative is involved in and necessary to the effective working of the judicial and must make a court within its proper scope a bureau of justice, not merely a machine for grinding out judgments and written opinions. Only by a gradual process did our law evolve a rational mode of trial for ascertainment of the facts of particular controversies. There may be an analogy here. Starting with purely mechanical modes of trying facts, the law developed rational methods. In the immediate past the social facts required for exercise of the judicial function of lawmaking have been arrived at by means which may fairly be called mechanical. In a transition from the mechanical lawmaking of the past century to rational lawmaking, not the least problem is to discover a rational mode of advising the court of facts of which it is supposed to take judicial notice.

What will be the effect of all these changes upon the spirit of our legal tradition—upon the spirit of the common law? They are so at variance with the course of our legal thought since the end of the seventeenth century that some fear our whole juristic edifice is about to be subverted. Yet the change of front today is no more radical than that which took place in the rise of the court of chancery, the development of equity and the consequent making over of the strict law by an infusion of morals. And the nineteenth century, after equity had been absorbed, could look back into the Year Books and recognize Choke and Brian and Fortescue, the worthies of our medieval law, as lights of the same system under which it was living. For through all vicissitudes the supremacy of law, the insistence upon law as reason to be developed by judicial experience in the decision of causes and the refusal to take the burden of upholding right from the concrete each and put it wholly upon the abstract all have survived. These ideas are realities in comparison whereof rules and dogmas are ephemeral appearances. They are so much a part of the mental and moral makeup of our race, that much more than legal and political revolutions will be required to uproot them.

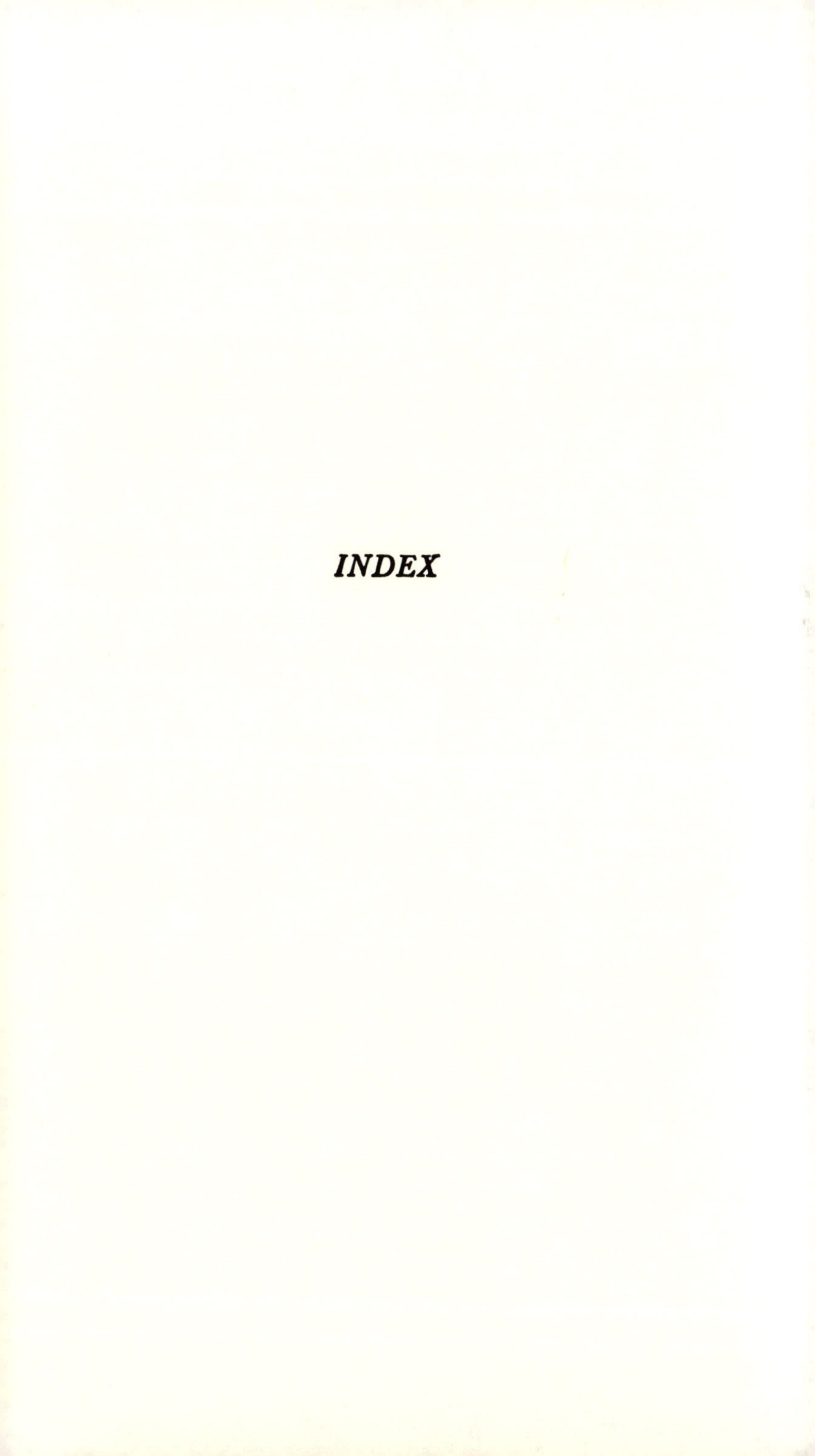

INDEX

INDEX

D

E

F